Imposter 22

Molly Davies

**Co-created with Kirsty Adams, Cian Binchy,
Housni Hassan (DJ), Dayo Koleosho, Stephanie Newman,
Lee Phillips and Charlene Salter**

From an original idea by Hamish Pirie

methuen | drama

LONDON • NEW YORK • OXFORD • NEW DELHI • SYDNEY

METHUEN DRAMA
Bloomsbury Publishing Plc
50 Bedford Square, London, WC1B 3DP, UK
1385 Broadway, New York, NY 10018, USA
29 Earlsfort Terrace, Dublin 2, Ireland

BLOOMSBURY, METHUEN DRAMA and the Methuen
Drama logo are trademarks of Bloomsbury Publishing Plc

First published in Great Britain 2023

Cover image by Paul Belford

Bloomsbury Publishing Plc does not have any control over, or responsibility
for, any third-party websites referred to or in this book. All internet addresses
given in this book were correct at the time of going to press. The author and
publisher regret any inconvenience caused if addresses have changed or sites
have ceased to exist, but can accept no responsibility for any such changes.

All rights whatsoever in this play are strictly reserved and application
for performance etc. should be made before rehearsals to LARK Management,
82 Rivington St, London EC2A 3AZ. No performance may be given unless a
licence has been obtained. No rights in incidental music or songs contained in
the Work are hereby granted and performance rights for any performance/
presentation whatsoever must be obtained from the respective copyright owners.

A catalogue record for this book is available from the British Library.

A catalog record for this book is available from the Library of Congress.

ISBN: PB: 978-1-3504-4772-1
ePDF: 978-1-3504-4773-8
eBook: 978-1-3504-4774-5

Series: Modern Plays

Typeset by Mark Heslington Ltd, Scarborough, North Yorkshire

To find out more about our authors and books visit
www.bloomsbury.com and sign up for our newsletters.

E ROYAL COURT THEATRE PRESENTS

Imposter 22

by Molly Davies

Co-created with Kirsty Adams, Cian Binchy, Housni Hassan (DJ), Dayo Koleosho, Stephanie Newman, Lee Phillips and Charlene Salter

From an original idea by Hamish Pirie

mposter 22 was first performed at the Royal Court Jerwood Theatre Downstairs, Sloane Square, on Saturday 23 September 2023.

poster 22

olly Davies

reated with Kirsty Adams, Cian Binchy, Housni Hassan (DJ), Dayo
osho, Stephanie Newman, Lee Phillips & Charlene Salter

n an original idea by Hamish Pirie

(in alphabetical order):
Kirsty Adams
Cian Binchy
(Alternate) **Anna Constable**
Housni Hassan (DJ)
Dayo Koleosho
Stephanie Newman
Lee Phillips
om **Charlene Salter**
y/Joe **Jamael Westman**

ctor **Hamish Pirie**
gner **Cai Dyfan**
ting Designer **Anna Watson**
nd Designer **XANA**
o Designer **Lewis den Hertog**
ement Director **Yami Löfvenberg**
stant Director **Aneesha Srinivasan**
se Coach **Christopher Holt**
stic Associate **Nick Llewellyn**
ge Manager **Verity Clayton**
uty Stage Manager **Fran O'Donnell**
istant Stage Manager **Adriana Perucca**
ative Support Workers **Kat Bond, Stella Farina, Gemma Harvey, Heather Johnson &**
ique Spencer
nd Operator **Florence Hand**
sser **Jennifer Mills**
erations **Anna Barcock**
built by **Ridiculous Solutions**

om the Royal Court, on this production:

age Supervisors **TJ Chappell-Meade & Steve Evans**
hting Supervisor **Max Cherry**
stume Supervisors **Katie Price & Lucy Walshaw**
oduction Manager **Marius Rønning**
und Supervisor **Jet Sharp**
mpany Manager **Mica Taylor**
ad Producer **Ralph Thompson**

poster 22 is a co-production with Access All Areas.

The Royal Court Theatre wish to thank the following for their help with this production:
Erica Campayne, Jonjo O'Neil, Brian Vernel.

Molly Davies (Writer)

For the Royal Court: **God Bless The Child, A Miracle.**

Other theatre includes: **Chicken (Eastern Angles/ Paines Plough Roundabout); Shooting Truth (National Theatre Connections); Orpheus & Eurydice (National Youth Theatre/Old Vic Tunnels); Magic (Paines Plough/Ipswich New Wolsey Theatre); Birds Stopped Singing (Company of Angels); The Future of Bump, Jenny Sings (Hampstead – heat&light and ESOL group); Things are Fragile (Shared Experience youth); The Best Team Since the A-Team (Southwark Playhouse youth); My Days (& Company of Angels), No Fairy Stories (Soho).**

Film includes: **TRUE THINGS.**

Awards include: **Harold Pinter Playwriting Award, Evening Standard Theatre Award for Most Promising Playwright (God Bless the Child), Westminster Prize (No Fairy Stories).**

Kirsty Adams
(Co-creator & Performer)

Kirsty is an actor, associate artist of Access All Areas, member of the Separate Doors National Ensemble and the BareFace Collective.

Theatre includes: **Fix Us (Lyric Hammersmith, Rosemary Branch, Soho, VAULT Festival and Edinburgh Fringe Festival); unReal City (Access All Areas, BAC & Brighton Dome in collaboration with dreamthinkspeak); Women Centre Stage (Hampstead).**

Other credits include: **Class Act.**

Awards include: **Shortlisted for the Pleasance Theatre Charlie Hartill Award (Fix Us).**

Kirsty graduated from Access All Areas' Performance Making Diploma at the Royal Central School of Speech and Drama.

Cian Binchy
(Co-creator & Performer)

Cian is an actor, writer, and associate artist of Access All Areas.

Theatre includes: **The Misfit Analysis (solo show with Access All Areas, Edinburgh Fringe/UK Tour/Mexico Tour with British Council); unReal City (Access All Areas, BAC & Brighton Dome in collaboration with dreamthinkspeak); MADHOUSE re:exit (Access All Areas, Lowry Theatre & Shoreditch Town Hall); Eye Queue Hear (Access All Areas, Rich Mix & UK Tour).**

Television includes: **Grace, Doctors, The Level.**

Awards include: **VAULT Festival People's Choice Award (The Misfit Analysis).**

Cian's consultancy work includes suppor the original development of "The Curious Incident of the Dog in the Night-Time" (National).

Cian graduated from Access All Areas' Performance Making Diploma at the Roya Central School of Speech and Drama.

Verity Clayton (Stage Manag

Theatre includes: **24 (Day): The Measure of my Dreams (Almeida); The Score(s) III (i.as.in. Barbican); Wuthering Heights (Inspector Sands/China Plate/Royal and Derngate/To Hamlet Reimagined (National); The Sorcer Apprentice (Northern Stage); Half Empty Glasses, The Ultimate Pickle, A Sudden Viol Burst of Rain (Rose/Paines Plough); Sorry You're not a Winner (Theatre Royal Plymou Paines Plough); The Storm Whale (& York Theatre Royal/Marlowe), The Journey Hom (& Beijing); Wow! Said the Owl (Little Angel/ Tour); The Snail and the Whale (Tall Stories/ West End/UK and International Tour); Unde the Rainbow (Polka/Tour).**

Anna Constable (Cast)

Anna is an actor and associate artist of Acc All Areas.

She graduated in 2023 from Access All Areas Performance Making Diploma at the Royal Central School of Speech and Drama.

This is Anna's first professional role, and sh honoured to be performing at the Royal Cou

Cai Dyfan (Designer)

For the Royal Court: **On Bear Ridge (& National Theatre Wales), Instructions For Correct Assembly, Violence and Son, Off The Page.**

As designer, other theatre includes: **The Village Socia Joseph K and the Cost of Living, The Passion (National Theatre Wales); Paul Bunyan (Welsh National Opera); Croendena, Imrie (Frân Wen); Trwy'r Ddinas Hon (Sherman); Sgint, Rhwng Dau Fyd, Chwalfa (Theatr Genedlaetho Cymru; After the End (Dirty Protest); Your Last Breath (Curious Detective); Wasted (Paines Plough/Birmingham Rep).**

As associate designer, other theatre includes: **The Lion, the Witch and the Wardrobe (Kensington Gardens); A Life of Galileo (RSC); A Number (Nuffield, Southampton); Mr Burns, King Charles III (& West End) (Almeida); Medea (National).**

As art director and buyer, television and film includes: **Willow, His Dark Materials, Apostle, Dal Y Mellt Hinterland/Y Gwyll, Y Swn, Wolf, Keeping Faith, A Discovery of Witches, Hidden/Craith, Born to Kill, Sherlock, Call the Midwife.**

~sni Hassan (DJ)
-creator & Performer)

an actor and dancer, an associate artist
ccess All Areas, Associate Artistic Director
nce company Corali, and a performer
cabaret collective Not Your Circus Dog.

re includes: **Not F**kin' Sorry (Soho & UK
)**; Duckie Presents – Princess (Royal
hall Tavern); unReal City (Access All Areas,
& Brighton Dome in collaboration with
mthinkspeak); MADHOUSE re:exit (Access
reas, Lowry Theatre & Shoreditch Town
; Eye Queue Hear (Access All Areas, Rich
& UK Tour).

e includes: **The People Race The Fish, Hearts
Faces, Origami Atoms (Corali); The Overlap
o show and National show); The Manifesto
a Perfect Cup of Tea (Solo show and
rnational tour).

graduated from Access All Areas'
formance Making Diploma at the Royal
tral School of Speech and Drama.

wis den Hertog
ideo Designer)

the Royal Court: **all of it.**

atre includes: **The Cherry Orchard (ETT/Yard);
acula, The Enemy, Panopticon, 306: Dusk
ational Theatre of Scotland); The Afflicted,
e Hope River Girls (groupwork); South Bend,
ry Play, Crude, Light Boxes (Grid Iron); We
e In Time (Raw Materials/Scottish String
semble); Wings Around Dundee, The Bridge,
e Snow Queen, The Cheviot, The Stag,
d The Black, Black Oil, The Tempest, Anna
renina (Dundee Rep).

hristopher Holt
/oice Coach)

eatre includes: **The Solid Life of Sugar Water
ational/Edinburgh/UK Tour); My Mother
aid I Never Should, Tribes (Sheffield); Cuttin'
(Royal Exchange); This Is Not For You, The
hreepenny Opera, Reason To Be Cheerful,
hiter Than Snow, Bent (Graeae).**

usic includes: **Better Late Than Never (John
elly).**

Vorkshops include: **Access All Areas, Springboard
Lyric Hammersmith), The Spotlight, Sphinx,
pen Age, Face Front, Actor's Centre, Arts
ducational Schools, Shared Experience,
amden Peoples' Theatre, Scoop.**

enior Lecturer at London Metropolitan
Jniversity, Fellow of the Higher Educational
cademy and Associate Theatre Facilitator
Outside Edge Theatre Company.

Dayo Koleosho
(Co-creator & Performer)

Dayo is an actor and associate artist of Access
All Areas, where he is also a trustee.

Theatre includes: **Faith, Hope and Charity
(National & international tour); Jitney
(Leeds Playhouse, Old Vic, Headlong UK tour);
#crazyfuturelove (Occupy Festival at BAC,
the Bubble Club and the Autism Arts Festival);
unReal City (Access All Areas, BAC & Brighton
Dome in collaboration with dreamthinkspeak);
MADHOUSE re:exit (Access All Areas, Lowry
Theatre & Shoreditch Town Hall); Eye Queue
Hear (Access All Areas, Rich Mix & UK Tour).**

Television includes: **Casualty, Strike, Grace,
Doctors, The Level, Damned, Holby City.**

Other credits include: **Paralympics Opening
Ceremony.**

Dayo founded collective duo 'Everyday Daylee'
with actor Lee Phillips.

Dayo graduated from Access All Areas'
Performance Making Diploma at the Royal
Central School of Speech and Drama.

Nick Llewellyn
(Artistic Associate)

Nick is the Artistic Director and CEO at
Access All Areas. He founded Access All
Areas' Performance Making Diploma at Royal
Central School of Speech and Drama, where
he is a visiting lecturer. Nick has devised and
directed numerous community shows for
Access All Areas' Black Cab Theatre alongside
the company's professional work, and was
previously Artistic Director at Hackney Shed.

Theatre includes: **unReal City (&
Dreamthinkspeak), The Interrogation (&
Lowry), MADHOUSE re:exit, The Misfit Analysis
(& Clan Binchy/international tour), Eye Queue
Hear, The Trial (& Retz) (Access All Areas/UK
tour).**

Yami Löfvenberg
(Movement Director)

For the Royal Court: **Living Newspaper, Rare Earth
Mettle.**

Other theatre includes: **Bird and Bees, Human
Nurture (Sheffield Theatres); UK Drill Project
(Barbican); Roundabout (Paines Plough); Kabul
Goes Pop (Brixton House); Athena (Yard);
Notes on Grief (Manchester International
Festival); Fuck You Pay Me (Bunker); Breakin'
Convention (Sadler's Wells); Talawa
TYPT (Hackney Showrooms).**

As director, theatre includes: **Fierce Flow** (Hippodrome, Birmingham); **Kind of Woman** (Camden People's); **Afroabelhas** (Roundhouse/British Council/Tempo Festival, Brazil).

As assistant director/assistant choreographer, theatre includes: **Hive City Legacy** (Roundhouse/HOME, Manchester/Millennium); **Hive City Legacy: Dublin** (Dublin Fringe).

Stephanie Newman
(Co-creator & Performer)

Stephanie is an actor, associate artist of Access All Areas, and a performer with cabaret collective Not Your Circus Dog.

Theatre includes: **Not F**kin' Sorry** (Soho & UK tour); **Duckie Presents – Princess** (Royal Vauxhall Tavern); **unReal City** (Access All Areas, BAC & Brighton Dome in collaboration with dreamthinkspeak); **Joy** (Royal Stratford East).

Stephanie graduated from Access All Areas' Performance Making Diploma at the Royal Central School of Speech and Drama.

Fran O'Donnell
(Deputy Stage Manager)

For the Royal Court: **What If, If Only, One for Sorrow, In the Republic of Happiness, Love and Information, Birthday, Cock, The Pride, Now or Later.**

Other theatre includes: **Dear England, Phaedra, Antony and Cleopatra** (National); **A Number, Girl from the North Country** (Old Vic); **A Doll's House Part 2** (Donmar); **The Winter's Tale, Harlequinade/All On Her Own, Red Velvet, The Painkiller, Romeo and Juliet, The Entertainer** (West End).

Lee Phillips
(Co-creator & Performer)

Lee is an actor, writer, facilitator, and associate artist of Access All Areas.

Theatre includes: **#crazyfuturelove** (Occupy Festival at Battersea Arts Centre, the Bubble Club and the Autism Arts Festival); **The Darkest Part of the Night** (Kiln); **unReal City** (Access All Areas, BAC & Brighton Dome in collaboration with dreamthinkspeak); **All Wrapped Up** (UK tour, Oily Cart).

Other credits include: **Training films for both NHS England and Resources for Autism.**

Lee graduated from Access All Areas' Performance Making Diploma at the Royal Central School of Speech and Drama.

He founded collective duo 'Everyday Dayle' with actor Dayo Koleosho.

Lee also performs with London Bubble, Sardines Dance, and Entelechy Arts.

Adriana Perucca
(Assistant Stage Manager)

Theatre includes: **Files** (Shoreditch Town Hall); **Paradise Now, The High Table, Strange Fruit** (Bush); **Things I Can Laugh About Now** (Brixton House); **Joan of Leeds** (New Diorama); **The Wolf of Wall Street Immersive Experience** (Specific, London); **Confirmation** (Pleasance, Edinburgh); **Bottom** (Soho); **Counting Sheep** (VAULT Festival), **Dangerous Giant Animals** (Theatre Row, New York).

Hamish Pirie (Director)

For the Royal Court: **Living Archive, Rare Earth Mettle, Living Newspaper, Listen Local** (Waltham Forest), **Instructions for Correct Assembly, Goats, Beyond the Court: Tottenham Primetime 2017, Human Animals, Violence & Son, Who Cares, Teh Internet is Serious Business.**

Other theatre includes: **Shibboleth** (Abbey, Dublin); **I'm with the Band** (& Wales Millennium Centre); **Quiz Show, Demos, 50 Plays for Edinburgh, Bravo Figaro** (& Royal Opera House) (Traverse); **Love With a Capital 'L', 3 Seconds, Most Favoured, The Last Bloom** (Traverse/Òran Mór); **Salt Root and Roe** (Donmar/Trafalgar Studios); **Stacy** (Arcola & Trafalgar Studios); **Purgatory** (Arcola); **Pennies** (nabokov); **Paper House** (Flight 5065).

Hamish trained as Resident Assistant Director at Paines Plough and at the Donmar Warehouse. He was previously Associate Director at the Traverse Theatre. Hamish is an Associate Director at the Royal Court.

Charlene Salter
(Co-creator & Performer)

Charlene is an actor, writer, facilitator, and associate artist of Access All Areas, where she is also co-chair of the board of trustees.

Theatre includes: **unReal City** (Access All Areas, BAC & Brighton Dome in collaboration with dreamthinkspeak); **The Interrogation** (solo show with Access All Areas & Lowry Theatre); **ZARA** (Mind the Gap).

Television includes: **Casualty, Doctors.**

Charlene graduated from Access All Areas' Performance Making Diploma at the Royal Central School of Speech and Drama.

s a facilitator on Access All Areas'
ultancy programmes, co-directed
ged (Access All Areas), and has worked
script development consultant for a
or broadcaster. She sits on the Creative
nerships Group board for BAC and was
ointed to the #FreelanceTaskForce.

eesha Srinivasan
ssistant Director)

he Royal Court: **Word-Play.**

rector, theatre includes: **Brown Girls Do It Too
-director] (& UK tour), Before I Was A Bear
Bunker) (Soho); The Woman in the Film
undhouse).**

ssistant director, theatre includes: **Name, Place,
mal, Thing (Almeida).**

na Watson (Lighting Designer)

the Royal Court: **Hope has a Happy Meal, That
lot Who I Am, Poet in da Corner (& UK tour),
of it, Pity, You for Me for You, Plaques and
agles, A Time to Reap.**

er theatre includes: **The Band's Visit,
propriate, Becoming: Part One, Salt Root
d Roe (Donmar); All of Us (National);
e Bolds, (Unicorn); The Winters Tale,
mlet, Henry VI, Richard III [as candlelight
nsultant] (Sam Wanamaker); Gaslight
atford Palace); The Nut Cracker, Christmas
rol (Bristol Old Vic); Leave to Remain,
e Seagull, Shopping & Fucking (Lyric,
ammersmith); The Fantastic Follies of
rs Rich, Snow in Midsummer, The Roaring
rl (RSC); Twilight: Los Angeles 1992, The
hronicles of Kalki (Gate); Box of Delights
Wilton's Music Hall); King Lear (Globe);
utchman, The Secret Agent, Fireface, Disco
gs, Sus (Young Vic); Bank on it (Theatre-
tes/Barbican); On the Record, it felt empty
hen the heart went at first but it is alright
ow (Arcola); Paradise, Salt (Ruhr Triennale,
ermany); Gambling, This Wide Night (Soho);
utherford and Son, Ruby Moon (Northern
tage); ...Sisters (Headlong); King Pelican,
peed Death of the Radiant Child (Drum,
lymouth).**

ance includes: **Merlin (Northern Ballet);
lothers, Soul Play (The Place); Refugees of
 Septic Heart (The Garage); View from the
hore, Animule Dance (Royal Opera House).**

pera includes: **Don Carlo (Grange Park); Orlando
Welsh National Opera/Scottish Opera/
an Francisco); Cendrillon (Gyndebourne);
Ruddigore (Barbican/Opera North/UK Tour);
Critical Mass (Almeida); Songs from a Hotel
Bedroom, Tongue Tied (Royal Opera House);
The Bartered Bride (Royal College of Music);
Against Oblivion (Toynbee Hall).**

Jamael Westman (Danny/Joe)

For the Royal Court: **Torn.**

Other theatre includes: **Patriots (Almeida);
Hamilton (West End/Eliza Tour); The Lorax (Old
Vic); The White Devil (Globe).**

Television includes: **Get Millie Black, The Essex
Serpent, Anne Boleyn, BBW.**

Film includes: **Good Grief, Munch, Animals.**

Awards include: **Evening Standard Theatre
Award's Emerging Talent Honour.**

XANA (Sound Designer)

For the Royal Court: **Word-Play, Living Newspaper
#4.**

Other theatre includes: **Anna Karenina (Edinburgh
Lyceum/Bristol Old Vic); Galatea (Emma
Frankland, Wildworks, Marlborough
Productions); Hamnet (RSC); The Trials, Mary
Seacole (Donmar); Sundown Kiki, Changing
Destiny, Fairview, Ivan and the Dogs, The
Collaboration (Young Vic); ...cake (Theatre
Peckham); Who Killed My Father (Tron/
Scotland tour); as british as a watermelon
(Contact); Hyde and Seek (Guildhall); Sleepova,
The P Word, Strange Fruit (Bush); Burgerz
(Hackney Showroom); Black Holes (The Place);
Sankofa: Before the Whitewash, Hive City
Legacy (Roundhouse); Glamrou: From Quran to
Queen, Curious, Half-Breed (Soho); Blood Knot
(Orange Tree); Noughts and Crosses (Pilot).**

Awards include: **Olivier Award for Outstanding
Achievement in an Affiliate Theatre 2023 (The
P Word).**

THE ROYAL COURT THEATRE

The Royal Court Theatre is the writers' theatre. It is a leading force in world theatre for cultivating and supporting writers – undiscovered, emerging and established.

Through the writers, the Royal Court is at the forefront of creating restless, alert, provocative theatre about now. We open our doors to the unheard voices and free thinkers that, through their writing, change our way of seeing.

Over 120,000 people visit the Royal Court in Sloane Square, London, each year and many thousands more see our work elsewhere through transfers to the West End and New York, UK and international tours, digital platforms, our residencies across London, and our site-specific work. Through all our work we strive to inspire audiences and influence future writers with radical thinking and provocative discussion.

The Royal Court's extensive development activity encompasses a diverse range of writers and artists and includes an ongoing programme of writers' attachments, readings, workshops and playwriting groups. Twenty years of the International Department's pioneering work around the world means the Royal Court has relationships with writers on every continent.

Since 1956 we have commissioned and produced hundreds of writers, from John Osborne to Jasmine Lee-Jones. Royal Court plays from every decade are now performed on stage and taught in classrooms and universities across the globe.

We strive to create an environment in which differing voices and opinions can co-exist. In current times, it is becoming increasingly difficult for writers to write what they want or need to write without fear, and we will do everything we can to rise above a narrowing of viewpoints.

It is because of this commitment to the writer and our future that we believe there is no more important theatre in the world than the Royal Court.

 royalcourt  royalcourttheatre

Supported using public funding by
ARTS COUNCIL
ENGLAND
ARTS COUNCIL ENGLAND

ROYAL

ASSISTED PERFORMANCES

ptioned Performances

ioned performances are accessible for people who are D/deaf, deafened & hard of
ing, as well as being suitable for people for whom English is not a first language.

oster 22
sday 12th October, 7:30pm

e Mist
rsday 9th November, 3pm
ay 10th November, 7:45pm

tes in Chelsea
dnesday 6th December, 7:30pm
rsday 7th December, 2:30pm

SL-interpreted Performances

L-interpreted performances, delivered by an interpreter, give a sign inteprretation of the
t spoken and/or sung by artists in the onstage production.

poster 22
day 13th October, 7:30pm

ates in Chelsea
turday 2nd December, 2:30pm

COURT

ASSISTED PERFORMANCES

Performances in a Relaxed Environment

Relaxed Environment performances are suitable for those who may benefit from a more relaxed environment.

During these performances:
- There is a relaxed attitude to noise in the auditorium; you are welcome to respond to the show in whatever way feels natural
- You can enter and exit the auditorium when needed
- We will help you find the best seats for your experience
- House lights may remain raised slightly
- Loud noises may be reduced

Imposter 22
All performances are relaxed.

Blue Mist
Saturday 11th November, 3pm

Mates in Chelsea
Saturday 9th December, 2:30pm

If you would like to talk to us about your access requirements, please contact our Box Office at (0)20 7565 5000 or boxoffice@royalcourttheatre.com

The Royal Court Visual Story is available on our website. Story and Sensory synposes are available on the show pages via the Whats On tab of the website shortly after Press Night.

CCESS
L AREAS

ess All Areas makes award-winning, disruptive performance by
'ning disabled and autistic artists.

productions create intimate moments of interaction between
formers and public, occupying unexpected spaces in venues, on
streets, online, and in public buildings.

well as making shows, our company of Associate Artists works to
ke our culture more inclusive for learning disabled and autistic
ent. We run access training, offer bespoke creative support to
rning disabled and autistic talent, and co-create scripts. We engage
nmunities, train artists of the future, and work closely with TV,
n, and theatre companies to make their work and workplaces more
cessible.

've developed a programme of work that challenges exclusion
every level of our culture. All our work, from productions, to
nsultancy, to training, to creative workshops, is co-led by Access All
eas' learning disabled and autistic artists, ensuring lived experience
ives everything we do.

llo@accessallareasproductions.org

:cessallareasproductions.org

‌OYAL COURT SUPPORTERS

‌r incredible community of supporters makes it possible for
‌ to achieve our mission of nurturing and platforming writers
‌every stage of their careers. Our supporters are part of our
‌sential fabric – they help to give us the freedom to take bigger
‌d bolder risks in our work, develop and empower new voices,
‌d create world-class theatre that challenges and disrupts
‌e theatre ecology.

‌ all our supporters, thank you. You help us to write the future.

‌BLIC FUNDING

‌HARITABLE PARTNERS

‌CORPORATE SPONSORS

‌CORPORATE MEMBERS

TRUSTS AND FOUNDATIONS

ROYAL

BAR & KITCHEN

The Royal Court's Bar & Kitchen aims to create a welcoming and inspiring environment with a style and ethos that reflects the work we put on stage.

Offering expertly crafted cocktails alongside an extensive selection of craft gins and beers, wine and soft drinks, our vibrant basement bar provides a sanctuary in the middle of Sloane Square. By day a perfect spot for meeting or quiet reflection and by night atmospheric meeting spaces for cast, crew, audiences and the general public.

All profits go directly to supporting the work of the Royal Court theatre, cultivating and supporting writers – undiscovered, emerging and established.

For more information, visit
royalcourttheatre.com/bar

HIRES & EVENTS

The Royal Court is available to hire for celebrations, rehearsals, meetings, filming, ceremonies and much more. Our two theatre spaces can be hired for conferences and showcases, and the building is a unique venue for bespoke events and receptions.

For more information, visit
royalcourttheatre.com/events

Sloane Square London, SW1W 8AS ⊖ Sloane Square ⇌ Victoria Station
🐦 royalcourt f theroyalcourttheatre ⊙ royalcourttheatre

COURT

t's be friends. With benefits.

Friends and Good Friends are part of the fabric of the Royal Court. y are our regulars and, together, we enjoy bold and restless theatre that vokes and challenges us all. Like all friends, they help us too. The income receive from our memberships directly supports our mission, providing ers with the space and platform to experiment and develop their writing.

ome a Friend today and inspire the next generation of theatre makers.

come a Friend (from £40 a year)

efits include:
- Priority Booking
- Advanced access to £12 Monday tickets
- 10% discount in our Bar & Kitchen and Samuel French bookshop

come a Good Friend (from £95 a year)

r Good Friends' membership also includes a voluntary donation. This extra pport goes directly towards supporting our work and future, both on and f stage.

addition to the Friend benefits, our Good Friends also receive:
- Five complimentary playtexts for Royal Court productions
- An invitation for two to step behind the scenes of the Royal Court Theatre at a special annual event

or more information, visit:
oyalcourttheatre.com/support–us

The English Stage Company at the Royal Court Theatre is a registered charity (No. 231242)

With thanks to:

Everyone at the Royal Court, especially Vicky, Ellie, Lucy, Jane and Aneesha. Nick, Lucy, Matt, Katie and Patrick at Access All Areas. Unique Spencer, Stella Farina, Heather Johnson, Kat Bond and Gemma Harvey. Fran O'Donnell, Adriana Perucca and Verity Clayton. Jonjo O'Neill and Brian Vernel. Lisa Jackson and Christian Sandino-Taylor. As always, thank you Michael Cox, Merle Cox Davies and Matty Cox Davies.

Imposter 22

For Anna, Cian, Charlene, Dayo, DJ, Jamael, Kirsty, Lee and Stephanie. And for Hamish. Thank you for your trust.

Characters

Blossom
Chloe
Geoff
Jake
Danny
Kev
Rose
Todd

Notes

A gap between words on a line like this   indicates a pause in speech; perhaps a searching for a word or thought.

. . . is a purposeful trailing off.

– indicates an interruption.

Danny (*playing* **Joe**) / **Danny** – *these are moments when there is a definite crossover between* **Danny** *and* **Joe***, or a shared feeling.*

The use of karaoke. In the first act, karaoke is used to help the characters reach an emotionally difficult moment for them in the reenactment. In the second act, they use it to explore Joe's emotional state. There wasn't time to clear the permissions needed to publish them, so instead I have detailed the artist, track and lines used.

Set. When the characters are puzzlers putting together the pieces of the story to get it straight, they should be in a separate area to when they are reenacting the story. In our production, there is a reenactment area, an octagon, in the middle of the stage, with a raised puzzler area around the outside with microphones. The monologue scenes were played on the forestage.

Act One

Scene One

Projected image of a handwritten note: What the ~~Audience~~ Witnesses Need to Know.

Kev *and* **Jake** *enter.* **Kev** *gives the audience a wave.*

Kev   This is a relaxed performance!

We don't mind about noise! We don't mind about walking around! Please! You must respond to the show in whatever way feels good! You must!

Feel free!

You are free!

You are welcome! You are welcome here.

This is for you.

Jake   Before we begin, I need to explain that you are not about to see the cabaret you were advertised. You are here to do a job. And your job is to be witnesses and actually properly listen for once in your lives. Because we need to get our story straight. Which doesn't mean making stuff up or lying. It means working out what happened in what order. And once we have worked out what happened it will prove we didn't do it. Then you will understand and can explain it to the police.

Kev   Yes, Jake! That's it! So my mum doesn't have to visit me in prison!

Jake   Because something only happened if a 'normal' saw it, as we know. I should define normal now, because it is a horrible word really and I think we all understand there is no such thing. For the purposes of our reenactment, a normal person is someone who is not excluded from what is accepted as everyday life due to their access needs.

Jake *looks carefully at the audience.*

The problem is. Yes, there is actually quite a. There's a surprising number of. There's a lot of learning disabled people out there.

Kev   Hello! Hi there!

Jake   That's OK. You can stay. But it doesn't really matter whether you're here or not, if you know what I mean. Oh I feel bad now. Anyway, that's our pre-show announcement finished so we are now ready to start.

Projected image of a handwritten note: Why We Are Here.

Blossom, **Chloe**, **Geoff**, **Rose** *and* **Todd** *enter.*

Todd   Ready Blossom? Ready Chloe, Ready Geoff? Ready Kev? Ready Rose?

Blossom, **Chloe**, **Geoff**, **Kev** *and* **Rose** *separately show* **Todd** *they are ready.*

Todd   What happened was, what happened was, this afternoon we went to our island in Battersea Park to check on Joe cos we hadn't seen him since yesterday when we left him there to go to karaoke in Margate. And we, when we got to the island, we realised he was dead and we wanted to find him and get him out of the water, we did, but

Blossom/Chloe/Geoff/Jake/Kev/Rose/Todd   Neenaw neenaw

Geoff   We fled the scene, we head for the hills!

Chloe   We called Rose's mum who picked us up in the van, Rose's mum said, 'You need to get your story straight.' She said, 'They will be knocking on our door any minute because neenaw neenaw and CCTV and number plates.'

Blossom   But we couldn't get our story straight because

Geoff   The light is on but nobody's home.

Kev   So so tricky! Telling! So tricky! Remembering! In order! The right way round!

Jake   The police will ask, no they will demand and shout and want details.

Blossom   We'll be sent down for years.

Geoff   Under lock and key.

Blossom   You can't escape people looking at you, in prison.

Todd   Always like, always be like supermarket security in there.

Geoff   Under surveillance.

Kev   The police are not here to be your friend!

Todd   You do not have to say anything. But it may harm your defence if you do not mention when questioned something that you later rely on in court. Anything you do say may be given in evidence.

Jake   I don't actually find that very clear.

Chloe   As we were being chased by the police in Rose's mum's van, I had my brainwave: we will reenact our time with Joe to prove we are innocent. We all just know our own bit of what happened. But if we put our own bit together with everyone else's then we will get the full picture. Like a jigsaw puzzle. I mean, the police reenact stuff all the time, why can't we?

Geoff   Beating them to it.

Kev   Geoff! That is the plan! That is the plan, my friend!

Chloe   We will be good at it cos we go to an acting group so we have all the skills. We just needed somebody to play Joe, and some witnesses who can tell the police.

Blossom   We thought about using an actor to play Joe. But actors are very expensive and we are all skint.

Todd   You have to, you do have to pay an actor the right amount or it is disrespectful.

Geoff   Equity. Unity is strength.

Rose   It couldn't be an actor anyway, because they would try to get all the focus on themselves, and the story we are getting straight is the story of me, basically.

Geoff   *Really?*

Jake   I wouldn't call it that. This is not the Rose Show.

Todd   Isn't it, isn't isn't it the Joe Show?

Chloe/Jake   No!

Jake   There isn't a main character.

Rose   Then it's not going to work. Someone will always force their way to the front and put themselves in the middle. Someone will always steal all the lines and action.

Blossom   Will someone really?!

Chloe   Anyway, we decided to look for a homeless man to play Joe instead. Cos we knew a homeless man would do as he is told and do anything for any money. And we knew it wouldn't be too difficult for him cos the homeless are used to talking to people they don't even know and doing speeches on the tube.

Jake   But as we sped along the streets looking for a homeless man between thirty and forty

Blossom/Chloe/Geoff/Jake/Kev/Rose/Todd   Neenaw neenaw

Jake   There the police were again. Luckily, they got distracted by all the, you know . . .

Geoff   Dodgy characters.

Jake   Doing extremely illegal highly suspicious things as we know. Doing far worse things than possibly fleeing a murder scene.

So, we drove the streets and found our man. Danny.

They all point to where **Danny** *should be.*

Jake   Danny! Danny!

Scene Two

Projection of a handwritten note which reads: 'Close-up on Chloe. Today 5.45pm'.

Chloe   We've got a hundred pounds? That could get you a tent or a night in a hotel or some of whatever it is you use. It was my idea to get one of you lot, that's why it's me doing the asking. The others are over there. See the white van? Rose's mum is driving.

We'll tell you everything we remember on the way. We'll tell you everything and you can make notes if you can write. And if you can read we'll use karaoke to help sometimes. Then you don't have to think what to say and you can dance. We will have a code word to stop the action if we need to, it's Jake's favourite TV character, an average teenage girl who lives a double life as a famous pop singer. We were at karaoke in Margate yesterday. Rose did the song choices, she knows everyone's favourites, it was wicked and then we came back and
saw
and
yeah

Do you ever see someone and think they look like they don't have worries? Like they never laugh at jokes they don't find funny and they must always be allowed to get to the end of their sentences. That must be good. Life must be simple for them.

This is kind of a big deal for me. Cos it's my idea and I don't have a lot of ideas. And it has to work or I don't know what will happen to us, that's the thing.

To get the money, all you have to do is exactly what we tell you. What do you think?

Scene Three

Continues from Scene One.

Jake   Danny!

Danny *enters from the opposite side of the stage to where the others pointed.*

Danny   OK so yeah.

Rose   And he is perfect.

Blossom   Apart from having no job and no home.

Todd   Getting the witnesses was easy because, it was easy because I knew, I knew this theatre didn't have a show on and so we could use it.

Chloe   We advertised this as a cabaret because everybody loves a learning disabled cabaret.

Todd   In the back of the van, Geoff did some posters, Rose put it on Facebook and Jake sent some tweets. And you came.

Jake (*to the other characters*)   At this point, I do think it is important to remember that my story might not be your story. I don't know if you did it. You don't know if I did it.

Blossom   None of us did it.

Jake   I can't prove I didn't do it if I don't know who did.

Chloe   It's OK, Jake. We will figure it out. Now, that's it I think. It's time to get our story straight. OK everybody, the stage is booked until 10pm, so take your time. No need to rush. We can all take our first positions.

Blossom   I just need to set my laptop up.

Todd   I can, I'll, I'll help you with that, Blossom.

Jake   Well, there is actually a need to rush, because as we all know, the police could turn up any minute.

Geoff   The clock is ticking.

Danny   OK so yeah, it would be good if we could speed things up cos I've got someone meeting me. He doesn't like to hang around and this has been a bit of a slow start.

Blossom   *Slow?*

Chloe   You just concentrate on looking at your notes, Danny. That's what you need to do if you want the money.

Rose *lifts* **Danny**'s *arm and reads it.*

Rose   The bus. It all started on the bus.

Chloe   That's right, Rose.

Geoff   The wheels on the bus go round and round.

Todd   So let's go back.

Geoff   Re-re-wind (*Like Craig David/Artful Dodger.*)

Kev   Exciting! Yes!

Scene Four

Blossom, **Chloe**, **Geoff**, **Jake**, **Kev**, **Rose** *and* **Todd** *stand behind a microphone. This is the position they take when they are not in one of the puzzle pieces.*

Danny *is in the area where the past is reenacted. Stage management have put out chairs to look like a bus.*

Todd (*to audience*)   This is a bus.

Geoff   The number 22.

Jake (*to the audience*)   It was the best they could do.

Todd   Time to meet some lovely people.

Kev   Connect! Connections, Todd! Yes!

Geoff   A window on the world.

Rose   I'd rather get an Uber.

Danny (*playing* **Joe**) *gets on the bus.*

Todd   Joe gets on the bus.

Geoff   Ooof.

Blossom   Joe didn't walk like that.

Todd   More upright, he was he was more upright. He didn't pull his sleeves down.

Danny (*playing* **Joe**) *gets off the bus.*

Danny   OK so yeah.

He changes his posture.

Better?

Chloe   Much better. Thank you, Danny. He doesn't have to be exactly the same as Joe, everybody.

Kev   Voice! His voice! Joe was from Crystal Palace!

Chloe   He's not gonna be one hundred per cent, Kev.

Danny   I could try . . . *like this?*

Blossom/Chloe/Geoff/Jake/Kev/Rose/Todd   No!

Kev   You are perfect just as you are, Danny! Perfect!

Geoff   Neenaw neenaw

Chloe   Yes, let's keep going.

Danny (*playing* **Joe**) *gets on the bus.*

Todd   Joe gets on the bus.

A shirt flies on from backstage.

Geoff   Snappy dresser.

Kev   Yeah, they just do that! They bring stuff on! Anything you want! Seriously! Anything! Any requests? Just ask me guys and I can do it. Well, they can! Anything!

Jake   He might be wearing a shirt but he is not going to work.

From this point on, characters can summon onto stage props and furniture that they would find useful. It could be a chaise longue. It could be roller skates, boxing gloves and a punch bag, binoculars, a megaphone, martial arts uniform or headphones.

Todd   Can we, can we have a spot on Joe, please.

A spotlight appears on **Joe**.

Todd   Joe is a history teacher with a, with a lanyard to prove it.

Rose *puts a lanyard on* **Danny** (*playing* **Joe**).

Jake   But he walked out of work today.

Kev   And he is not going to his dentist appointment either. No! I don't think he even cares about his teeth right now!

Rose   He is not going to see his girlfriend because he doesn't live with her anymore because she isn't his girlfriend anymore.

Todd   You can tell. You can tell by his head down. You can tell by his eyes down that he's he's, uh

Danny (*playing* **Joe**) *lowers his head and eyes.*

Jake   Yes, he's, he's very. He looks quite

Todd   He uh

Todd *gets on the bus and stands opposite* **Danny** (*playing* **Joe**).

Todd *hugs* **Danny** (*playing* **Joe**).

Blossom, Chloe, Geoff, Jake, Kev *and* **Rose** *study* **Todd** *and* **Danny** (*playing* **Joe**).

Kev/Chloe/Geoff   Ahhhhh.

Geoff   Sweet.

Blossom   They're having A Moment.

Jake   Yes, it is very nice. And I know exactly what is going on here.

Geoff   Break this down, Jake. Get close up.

Jake   Yes, what is going on here is Joe's serotonin levels are increasing to make him feel all happy and calm. There will be endorphins racing round his body. They are basically the same as painkillers but much better as they are thirty times more effective and not as addictive. Speaking of addiction, this hug will be releasing the hormone oxytocin which will lower Joe's heart rate and any feelings of stress he might have and which also *lessens cravings for drugs and alcohol.* Which might be of interest to you, Danny.

Geoff   Hugs not drugs.

Jake   Whilst I do understand all of this about hugs, most of the time I don't really feel it. Most of the time when someone comes to hug me, I feel a surge of energy propelling me away, like an electric shock. That's not what is happening here though, clearly.

Blossom   Here, they are swapping energies. Todd is giving Joe his strength.

Chloe   Yeah, this isn't the kind of hug that traps you. Like when someone says 'Go on, give Aunty a hug' and her perfume makes your eyes water and her hair gets in your mouth. That is a bad hug. But this, this is a good hug.

Geoff   Just what the doctor ordered.

Rose   OK, that's enough now.

Todd *breaks out of the hug and gets off the bus.*

Geoff   A new man.

Rose   He looks better.

Chloe   He looked like he wanted to, you know, not be not be here. But now . . .

Geoff   He's staying alive!

Kev   Todd made things better!

Todd   Now Todd is now Todd's gone.

Danny *checks his arm.*

Danny (*playing* **Joe**)   Wait!

Danny (*playing* **Joe**) *gets off the bus. He approaches* **Blossom**.

Danny (*playing* **Joe**)   Excuse me. I don't want a Big Issue, thanks so much. I'm looking for this man?

Blossom   HANNAH MONTANA! Hang on a minute. Did Todd see Joe do this? It might not be right.

Rose   Todd, did you?

Todd   Uh I don't   no, I don't,   I'm not sure.

Blossom   Then this is guesswork.

Geoff   An educated guess.

Jake   Yes that is right, Geoff. Sometimes the police make educated guesses.

Todd   The police don't have much training, some are not too good, not too good at their jobs.

Chloe   That is very true, Todd. We will be more thorough though.

Jake   Well, they are about to turn up *any minute* so shall we continue?

Chloe   Blossom?

Blossom   OK, fine. Keep going.

Danny (*playing* **Joe**)   Hi. I'm looking for this man. He's uh, he's about this tall. He's Black, he's wearing a dark blue hoodie. And red trainers, he's wearing red trainers.

Blossom   He went that way.

Danny (*playing* **Joe**)   That way. Right. OK.

Oh, here.

Danny (*playing* **Joe**) *gives* **Blossom** *a coin.*

Geoff   Big mistake!

Kev   No, Joe! What a sucker!

Chloe   I hope he hid his phone away.

Blossom   You know, you lot don't have to believe every warning you're given.

Chloe   So what happened next?

Todd   Joe must have seen, seen me. From a distance.

Todd *enters the reenactment area.* **Danny** (*playing* **Joe**) *'sees' him.*

Blossom   Maybe Joe was a stalker?

Kev   Was Joe a baddie? I'm not sure.

Geoff   Maybe baby. Maybe.

Chloe   Not until later. It's what we are seeing right now we need to focus on. Any ideas anybody?

Jake   Maybe he was Todd's lover?

Rose   He was not Todd's lover.

Jake   It is best to keep an open mind, Rose.

Rose   I'm telling you, he was not Todd's lover.

Jake   Could Joe have been depressed, I'm wondering?

Blossom   Or *impressed*, with Todd?

Kev   That's it, Blossom! That's it, I think. Look, guys, look, he's getting closer!

Geoff   Gaining ground.

Chloe   I think he's trying to steal something.

Blossom   Yeah, he's trying to steal something from Todd.

Kev   He's going to mug him! Oh no!

Danny (*playing* **Joe**) *reaches out to* **Todd**.

Danny (*playing* **Joe**)   Hello. I'm Joe.

Kev   Yes, Joe! Hi, Joe!

Danny (*playing* **Joe**)   What's your name?

Todd   Uh. Do I, do I know you?

Danny (*playing* **Joe**)   No. But I feel like you know me, if that makes sense? My name's Joe. What's yours?

Todd   Uh   I don't know   if I should tell you.

Danny (*playing* **Joe**)   We met on the bus just now. The 22? Do you remember?

Todd   Uh

Danny (*playing* **Joe**)   You came up and gave me a hug. I'd been feeling quite. Very.

Jake   You can see where this going a mile off.

Danny (*playing* **Joe**)   But then you hugged me and I felt, I think actually maybe you

Jake   Oh Joe, don't be that person!

Danny (*playing* **Joe**)   I think you sort of saved me.

Jake   There we go.

Geoff   Classic.

Blossom   Next he'll say, you made me realise how lucky I am blah blah blah.

Danny (*playing* **Joe**)   I was feeling. But then you hugged me and – this is so full-on, sorry – then you hugged me and for a moment I got a glimpse of something. Sort of another way to be, I suppose. And I stopped feeling how I've been feeling. I know this sounds, but I wanted to see you again. So, I followed you.

Todd   I hug a lot of people on the 22.

Geoff   Ooof, gutted!

Jake   You are not special. I repeat, you are not special.

Danny (*playing* **Joe**)   Oh, OK.

Todd   They all uh they all   look the same   a lot of the time. Sorry.

Danny (*playing* **Joe**)   So you don't remember?

Todd   Maybe. I don't know. I'm confused.

Danny (*playing* **Joe**)   No, that's OK.

Blossom   Of course it's OK. He knows it's OK. He doesn't need you to tell him that.

Jake   You are very angry, aren't you Blossom? You are very angry with Joe. Can't say I blame you, but it is worth noting, (*To the audience.*) if you know what I mean?

Blossom   I'm not angry, I'm tired.

Danny (*playing* **Joe**)   Is it alright if I walk with you?

Todd   I have to go somewhere. I uh I was just going somewhere.

Danny (*playing* **Joe**)   Where?

Chloe   Joe is going to make Todd late in a minute, you know.

Todd   To my group.

Danny (*playing* **Joe**)   What kind of group?

Todd   Acting.

Danny (*playing* **Joe**)   Like, a class?

Todd   Uh huh.

Danny (*playing* **Joe**)   I've not done any acting since I was a kid.

Todd   Oh.

Danny (*playing* **Joe**)   Is it good?

Todd   Uh yeah, it is.

Danny (*playing* **Joe**)   Could I walk with you, to the class?

Todd   I don't know. I   get the Tube.

Danny (*playing* **Joe**)   Could I walk to the station with you then?

Todd   I don't know.

Danny (*playing* **Joe**)   Cool. So look, I wouldn't normally do this. I just get a very strong feeling that I shouldn't be alone at the minute.

Geoff   Honesty is the best policy.

Kev   Don't Joe, don't be alone! He's lonely!

Jake   I bet you're feeling quite bad now, Blossom. I bet you're feeling all sorry for Joe and maybe a little bit regretful?

Blossom   I didn't kill him, Jake.

Todd   My name my my my name is   Todd.

Danny (*playing* **Joe**)   Can we walk together, Todd?

Todd   I'm going to get the Tube.

Pause.

Danny (*playing* **Joe**)   We could walk to the station together?

Todd   I don't know. I just met you. I don't know.

Danny (*playing* **Joe**)   I'll travel with you. We can talk on the way. What do you think?

Blossom *plays Rihanna 'Russian Roulette' on the karaoke app on her laptop. The lyrics of the last two lines of the first verse appear on a screen.*

Kev   Nice choice, Blossom, nice. That's yours, Rose! That's one of yours!

Rose   Yes, it is.

Geoff   The top three.

Danny (*playing* **Joe**)   What do you think?

Todd   You seem nice but   maybe. OK, yeah.

OK yeah alright.

Jake (*to the audience*)   So far so familiar, eh: a sad little neurotypical is made to feel better after meeting a smiley happy learning disabled guy.

Chloe   What line do you take to acting, Todd?

Todd   Jubilee line, I take I take the Jubilee line.

Chloe   OK, let's do that then. Well done for getting this far everybody. Let's keep remembering why we are here, OK.

Geoff   Neenaw neenaw, eyes on that prize.

Scene Five

Todd *and* **Danny** (*playing* **Joe**) *sit on a Jubilee line train. In silence.*

Danny (*playing* **Joe**)   Do you look at all the other people and wonder where they're going? I like to do that.

Todd   I like to I like to listen, I like listening to the announcements.

Danny (*playing* **Joe**)   Or maybe you're not fussed about other people that much?

Todd   I I I I listen I listen to the announcements.

Danny (*playing* **Joe**)   When there's no announcement, though? Like now.

Todd   I wait so I don't miss anything I don't miss anything when the announcement comes.

Danny (*playing* **Joe**)   Do you tend to think about other people or your own stuff or. Yeah, what do you think about?

Todd   I   tend   not to speak on the Tube.

Danny (*playing* **Joe**)   Cool, yeah that's fine. I can do that.

They sit in silence.

Scene Six

The reenactment area is the acting class.

Chloe (*to the audience*)   Last year, I did training through our theatre company to be a workshop leader.

Todd   She is really, she she is really good at it.

Chloe   Thanks, Todd. Joe came in just as the session was starting.

Blossom, **Chloe**, **Geoff**, **Jake**, **Kev**, **Rose**, **Todd** *and* **Danny** (*playing* **Joe**) *are in the class at the top of the scene.*

Chloe   Thank you everyone. That was a great warm-up. Our first exercise today is mirroring in pairs. So, so, so, so yeah I'm gonna put you into pairs.

She puts them in pairs – **Geoff** *and* **Jake**; **Rose** *and* **Todd**; **Danny** (*playing* **Joe**) *and* **Blossom**.

Chloe   A, B, A, B, A, B. Kev we can go together and you can be A. A will be leading and B will be following.

You remember mirroring? Think of using different levels and of speed, using different speeds. When you're ready you can start.

The performers mirror one another.

Quiet concentration.

Blossom *is centre stage, being copied by* **Danny** *(playing* **Joe***). It's different to how everyone else is mirroring though; he's not just copying what she's doing, he's copying* her.

Blossom *is suspicious. This isn't how it usually feels doing mirroring. She stops. She tries to speak but every time she opens her mouth,* **Danny** *(playing* **Joe***) does the same.*

Blossom   Are you taking the piss?

Danny *(playing* **Joe***)* *(imitating* **Blossom***'s voice)*   Are you ta ta taaaking the piss?

Blossom/Danny *(playing* **Joe***)*   Are you ta ta taaaking the piss?

Blossom   St/op

Danny *(playing* **Joe***)*   Stop!

Blossom/Danny *(playing* **Joe***)*   STOP!

Chloe   Blossom, is everything OK?

Blossom   He's copying me.

Chloe   That's because we're doing mirroring.

Blossom   He wasn't copying properly, though. Did you see? He got too close. He tried to do my face, he did my voice. It felt like he was trying to get inside my head. I don't even know who he is.

Danny *(playing* **Joe***)*   I'm Joe.

Kev   Hi, Joe!

Danny (*playing* **Joe**)   Hi. Look, I apologise if I've done anything wrong, I thought I was engaging in the exercise we were given to do. I was just trying to do it well.

Jake   What made you think that you would be right for this group, Joe, if I may ask?

Danny (*playing* **Joe**)   Sorry, how do you mean?

Jake   I mean, not anyone can join this group. What made you think you could?

Danny (*playing* **Joe**)   Well, when Todd mentioned it, it was funny because it was something I'd always wanted to do.

Chloe   Did you get a referral?

Danny (*playing* **Joe**)   Did I? I can't re – No, yeah, I think I did.

Chloe   You need a referral to join our group.

Danny (*playing* **Joe**)   That's it, I got a referral from, yeah.

Chloe   There's a register. Did you see, at the front desk? Luke, he does all that. I can't do that.

Danny (*playing* **Joe**)   His computer was being slow, he said to go in and he'd sort it out afterwards because the class was starting. Sorry, have I done something wrong?

Chloe   No, Joe, don't worry.

Kev   No worries, Joe.

Jake   But you should know, we have rules in this group, Joe.

Kev   Uh huh, we have rules we do we do have rules, Joe.

Jake   The main one being respect.

Geoff   Do unto others as you would have them do unto you.

Rose   You should bow to Geoff, he's a sensei.

Danny (*playing* **Joe**) *bows.* **Rose** *checks him out.*

Blossom   Did you see what he was doing? Did you see?

Chloe   We don't usually copy each others voices and stuff. It's not respectful.

Danny (*playing* **Joe**)   Sorry. I didn't know.

Blossom   I'm not lying!

Chloe   No one thinks that.

Kev   He didn't know, Blossom! He didn't know the rules!

Blossom   He was taking the piss.

Danny (*playing* **Joe**)   I really wasn't.

Blossom   I'm telling you. He thinks I didn't realise.

Chloe   Blossom, do you want to take a minute? A bit of time outside? Some water or anything?

Blossom   I don't know.

Chloe   I think you should have some time outside.

Blossom *puts Kate Bush 'This Woman's Work' on the karaoke.*

Blossom *sings half way through the second and the third line of the first chorus.*

Blossom   Yeah alright, yeah actually I do need a minute.

Blossom *leaves.*

Jake   I would like to know why Joe wanted to be in this group. Because there are lots of different things you can be referred to join, Joe.

Danny (*playing* **Joe**)   Yeah, true. Definitely. So, I met Todd and we connected and that was amazing and I thought, I would like to think like him because

Yeah, it really came at the right moment cos I've been feeling very separate, from other people recently?

Like they have felt far away and further along somehow.
Like they have all the answers when the answers have been
escaping me, when all I have is questions?

So yeah, to have a connection with someone was bliss and I'd
like more of that I guess. I feel like I've got a lot to learn
from you all. Yeah, I'm loving the group so far.

Todd   That, that makes that does make, that does make
sense to me.

Geoff   How very interesting.

Kev   It is! It is! Of course! Of course you can join Joe!
Welcome!

Jake   Hearing you put it like that, yes, it does make quite a
lot of sense, I suppose. Yes, I'd like to welcome you to the
group as well, Joe.

Danny (*playing* **Joe**)   Thank you.

Chloe   Right so we had all met him by this point.

Blossom   But only some of us could see who he really was.

Chloe   Don't blame yourself though, if you didn't. After all,
none of us could tell what was going to happen.

Scene Seven

By Dayo and Lee and Molly.

*Projection of a handwritten note which reads: 'Close-up on Geoff
and Todd, The Future'.*

Geoff   Money sometimes makes me funny
Don't want to seem greedy, want to give it to the needy
My brother he say stop it,
pretend like you don't got it
Tell a lie, say you're broke
Listen this ain't no joke.

Geoff/Todd   My brother he knows the ropes (x2)

Todd   My Freedom Pass went missing on the train
How did I lose it, man I feel like such a pain
Damn I am so careless, I know you think I'm reckless
But me and Gee we are famous,
I can see that makes you jealous.

Geoff/Todd   It's not always easy to see, not to me
what that look upon their face is
are they showing true, false,
what's the case
Mando standing in the shadows
disrupting our flow,
is he evil dangerous baddie
or just a goodie in a hoodie?

Geoff/Todd   My brother he knows the ropes (x2)

Geoff   and one day, like him, I know
there will be no flies on me I hope.

Geoff/Todd   My brother he knows the ropes.

Scene Eight

The reenactment area is outside the acting class.

Chloe   So Rose and me were just talking. Rhubarb rhubarb.

Rose   Rhubarb.

Danny (*playing* **Joe**) *enters the reenactment area.*

Danny (*playing* **Joe**)   Hey, hey, Chloe.

Chloe   Uh, yeah?

Danny (*playing* **Joe**)   Where's Todd?

Chloe   He left, I think when you were talking to Luke
just now.

Danny (*playing* **Joe**)   Oh no, I wanted to go with him. What are you both up to?

Chloe   Going home.

Danny (*playing* **Joe**)   Shall we get some of the others together? We could all go on somewhere?

Chloe   No. I can't do that. I need to go home.

Bye, Rose.

Rose   Bye.

Chloe   Actually no I. Actually I, I, I want to say something.

Danny (*playing* **Joe**)   Please, do.

Chloe   There's a lot of trust in this group.

Danny (*playing* **Joe**)   I can see. I can really see that. It's lovely.

Chloe   Yeah, so why are you here?

Danny (*playing* **Joe**)   How do you mean?

Chloe   I mean –

Danny (*playing* **Joe**)   I really wasn't mocking Blossom.

Todd   He needs, he needs to let her finish.

Chloe   But something isn't something's not right.

Danny (*playing* **Joe**)   Not right? How do you mean?

Chloe   I'm not sure, I mean / why you're here.

Danny (*playing* **Joe**)   I'm just trying to connect with new people. To learn new things.

Jake   'Enlighten me, enlighten me.' Poor little neurotypical.

Kev   That's not fair! Is it? That's not Joe!

Blossom   Are you saying Chloe's lying, Kev? And why didn't you lot stick up for me more back there?

Geoff   The benefit of the doubt.

Blossom   You've known me for a year. You'd only known him a few hours.

Danny (*playing* **Joe**)   Is that bad? To want to connect with people? To want to keep learning?

Chloe   . . . No.

Danny (*playing* **Joe**)   Am I a bad person? I don't know.

Chloe   I don't think you are doing / anything bad.

Danny (*playing* **Joe**)   You must tell me if I offended you.

Blossom   It's not her job to explain it to you. You do some work.

Danny (*playing* **Joe**)   You must let me know, if I have.

Blossom   Educate yourself, man.

Chloe   You haven't offended me.

Blossom   He has.

Danny (*playing* **Joe**)   That's a relief. I'd love to come again next week, if I'm around.

Chloe   OK.

Danny (*playing* **Joe**)   So, we're all good?

Chloe   . . . Yeah

Danny (*playing* **Joe**)   Great.

Chloe   I've got to – Bye.

Chloe *rushes off.*

Geoff   Rose and Joe, all alone.

Todd   What could, what could possibly happen now?

Rose   Hello.

Danny (*playing* **Joe**)   Hi.

Rose   I'm Rose.

Danny (*playing* **Joe**)   Hi, Rose.

Rose   Hi, Joe. Would you like to marry me?

Danny *looks at his arm.*

Rose   He said yes of course, so then we went back to mine.

Chloe   So let's do Rose and Joe on the Tube. We need the Tube on again.

Blossom   Rose would have her headphones on from the minute she sat down. She likes to watch reruns of Neighbours when she's on public transport.

Jake   Wearing headphones doesn't make Rose innocent of killing Joe.

Geoff   Anything is possible.

Chloe   Rose, what happened when you were on the Tube with Joe?

Rose   Helen Daniels was kidnapped.

Blossom   See?

Chloe   Nothing else, Rose?

Rose   She was held captive in a shed at Erinsborough Cemetery by Reverend Errol Price whose real name was Ralph Drew because he was actually a phoney.

Chloe   OK. We won't do the journey.

Todd   Right then, everyone back to, everyone back to Rose's.

Scene Nine

The reenactment area is **Rose**'s *house.*

Rose   There is a chair there and a sofa here. We need those.

Kev (*calling back stage*)   A chair, please! A sofa!

A chair and sofa arrive. **Rose** *and* **Joe** *sit down.*

Rose   Are you into music?

Danny (*playing* **Joe**)   Yeah, yeah I am. Are you?

Rose   Yes.

Rose's *phone buzzes.*

I love music.

Danny (*playing* **Joe**)   What kind?

Rose   All kinds.

Danny (*playing* **Joe**)   I like sort of bluesy stuff and –

Rose   My top three songs are Susan Boyle doing 'I Dreamed a Dream', 'Time to say Goodbye' by Andrea Bocelli and Sarah Brightman, and Rihanna 'Russian Roulette'.

Rose's *phone buzzes.*

Danny (*playing* **Joe**)   Do you like making lists then? Of your favourite things?

Rose   No. Number four is The Shires, 'Daddy's Little Girl'. Some of my friends like lists. I'm not fussed though.

Danny (*playing* **Joe**)   Right. I see.

Rose   Geoff's top three artists are the Notorious B.I.G., Tupac and Drake. Blossom's are The Strokes, Jack White and Arcade Fire.

Danny (*playing* **Joe**)   Yeah, I can tell you're really not into lists.

Rose   Shut up!

Rose's *phone buzzes again.*

Rose   Omigod. Leave me alone.

Danny (*playing* **Joe**)   Who's that?

Rose   My other boyfriend. Joking. It's my mum.

Danny (*playing* **Joe**)   She messages a lot.

Rose   Because I'm not replying. I need to reply.

She types on her phone.

H-o-m-e.

My parents are overprotective.

Danny (*playing* **Joe**)   My mum can be like that.

Rose   Because you were dropped on your head as a baby?

Danny (*playing* **Joe**)   Because she worries that I might disappear or something.

Rose   Will you disappear?

Danny (*playing* **Joe**)   I'm not sure.

Do you ever want to?

Rose   No.

Danny (*playing* **Joe**)   No, of course not.

Blossom   Why of course not?

Rose   I'm going to be here forever.

Kev   I bet she is as well. Go, Rose!

Danny (*playing* **Joe**)   I chucked my phone in the end, it got too annoying.

Rose   Oh.

Danny (*playing* **Joe**)   Threw it in the river.

Rose   That wasn't very sensible.

Danny (*playing* **Joe**)   What do you do then, when things start to get to you?

Rose   Nothing.

Danny (*playing* **Joe**)   Nothing like you ignore stuff, let it wash over you, or nothing like nothing really gets you down too much?

Rose   I don't know.

Danny (*playing* **Joe**)   Sometimes I get on a bus and see what happens, where it will take me. I don't check the number or direction. I want to get lost I suppose.

Rose   Oh.

Danny (*playing* **Joe**)   Do you ever do that?

Rose   No.

Danny (*playing* **Joe**)   No.

Rose   Sometimes I go to our island if everything is getting too noisy.

Danny (*playing* **Joe**)   What island?

Rose   Joe.

Danny (*playing* **Joe**)   Rose.

Rose   Do you have a girlfriend?

Danny (*playing* **Joe**)   No.

Rose   Good.

Danny (*playing* **Joe**)   I need to move my stuff out of the flat. Shit. No, not anymore.

Rose   Joe, you're an amazing man.

Danny (*playing* **Joe**)   I'm not.

Rose   Joe, you're a handsome man. You're even better than Joe Wicks.

Geoff   Classic EastEnders character. Absolute classic.

Chloe (*to the audience*)   I know it is very important to Rose that you understand this is not the, you know, the fitness guy she is talking about.

Geoff   The Body Coach.

Chloe   Yeah, it's not him.

Rose I love your eyes and I love the way you walk. I'd like to hold your hand.

Rose *puts out her hand.*

Danny (*playing* **Joe**) OK . . .

Danny (*playing* **Joe**) *takes it. They hold hands.*

Danny (*playing* **Joe**) This is nice.

Rose I'd like to kiss you now and I'd like you to kiss me back.

Danny (*playing* **Joe**) OK.

Rose That is why I brought you here.

Danny (*playing* **Joe**) Have you kissed anyone before?

Rose Yes. Sometimes on a Tuesday I kiss someone.

Danny (*playing* **Joe**) Always a Tuesday?

Rose On Tuesdays I go to acting and come home by myself and my parents do the food shop. So there's time.

Geoff Seizing her window of opportunity with both hands.

Danny (*playing* **Joe**) Do you just go to the acting class or other groups too?

Rose But tonight they are going to a party after the food shop so they won't be back until morning. Do you want to kiss me?

Danny (*playing* **Joe**) Do I want to kiss you?

Rose Yes.

Danny (*playing* **Joe**) Do you want me to kiss you?

Rose Yes.

Danny (*playing* **Joe**) I do want to kiss you.

Chloe This was a private moment, we don't need to see it. I don't think it will give us any clues.

Blossom It could do, Chloe, we don't know.

Todd   Is it allowed?

Blossom   *Allowed?*

Kev   Is it, Blossom? What will the police think? What will they (*The audience.*) think?

Chloe   OK, we do need to see it.

Rose   They are going to be out all night not all week so you should do it now.

Danny/Danny (*playing* **Joe**) *moves to put his hand on* **Rose**'*s knee.*

Rose '*pauses*' *him.*

She picks up a microphone.

Geoff   It's happening, people.

Blossom   Here we go.

Rose   Stroke my hair first.

Joe does as I say and my hair is soft as silk between his fingers. I pull him close and kiss him with my excellent kissing. Then I perform some ballroom dancing and he gets to watch.

Blossom   Rose is a fantastic dancer.

Kev   She really is.

Rose   He also gets to watch me take my clothes off and I'm jealous because he can see me from all angles everywhere. I only get to see myself in the mirror but even then I'm magnificent. I'm magnificent as I run my hands down. Down his neck down his chest down his tummy down his penis and up his penis and I hold his penis and my hands are soft because I never wash up and firm because I'm young and wet because I'm sweating and that is a good combination. I'm even better at this than at kissing and his face and his breath and his noises mean he doesn't want me to stop but I do stop because looking isn't enough for me and touching isn't enough for me. I want more. I want it all.

So I tell him to sit down on the sofa but first I take the cushions off for myself because floor boards are too hard to kneel on and I am kissing and tasting his penis with my tongue and my mouth which is like a lovely soft slipper sock. I lie on the cushions and pull him on top of me and we are so, so close but I need him to be even closer. I tell Joe to get the condom I always carry in my coat pocket and I lie back and watch as he puts it on. He is glowing and glistening and he can't take his eyes off me and I want him in my nose in my ears in my vagina and he looks down at my beautiful face like Jack looks down at Rose in the car on the Titanic and –

Danny (*playing* **Joe**)   Oh.

Jake   Oh.

Blossom   Huh? What's going on?

Rose   This didn't happen in Titanic.

Danny (*playing* **Joe**)   No.

It's not

I'm sorry.

Kev   Not your fault, Joe.

Danny (*playing* **Joe**)   I'm on this medication and it can stop, well, it makes this happen. Not happen. Oh god, I should have mentioned before. Sorry.

Rose   Are you sick?

Danny (*playing* **Joe**)   They're antidepressants.

For depression.

Rose   Obviously.

Danny (*playing* **Joe**)   Obviously. So I don't think we're going to be able to, I don't think it's going to work.

Rose   OK.

They get a bit more comfortable on the sofa.

Budge over, you're taking up all the room.

Danny (*playing* **Joe**)   That better?

Rose   Ouch, you're on my hair.

Jake (*playing* **Rose**'s *dad*; *off*)   We're home!

Danny (*playing* **Joe**) *leaps up.*

Danny (*playing* **Joe**)   Shit, who's that?

Rose   My dad. My parents.

Danny (*playing* **Joe**)   You said they were out all evening.

Rose   I wanted you to stay.

Danny (*playing* **Joe**)   OK. Oh God. OK. Let's just act normal. Quick, Rose.

Rose   Don't rush me.

Chloe (*playing* **Rose**'s *mum*) *and* **Jake** (*playing* **Rose**'s *dad*) *enter.*

Chloe (*playing* **Rose**'s *mum*)   Oh. Hello.

Danny (*playing* **Joe**)   Hello.

Rose   This is Joe. My boyfriend. Don't start.

Danny (*playing* **Joe**)   I don't think we decided –

Rose   We met at Acting. We're in love, basically.

Jake (*playing* **Rose**'s *dad*)   Hello, Joe. From the acting group? Do we know your parents?

Rose   Omigod. I said don't start!

Chloe (*playing* **Rose**'s *mum*)   We are not starting, Rose. We are just getting to know your new friend.

Rose   *Boyfriend.*

Chloe (*playing* **Rose**'s *mum*)   Well, Joe doesn't seem sure he is your boyfriend.

Rose   Because you are scaring him.

Chloe (*playing* **Rose**'s *mum*)   We aren't scary!

Jake (*playing* **Rose**'s *dad*)   Let's use the word friend for now as it's more comfortable for everybody.

Rose   Sure, whatever, maybe you think I have sex with all my friends.

Jake (*playing* **Rose**'s *dad*)   Oh Rose, enough please. Joe, would you like a cup of tea?

Danny (*playing* **Joe**)   No thank you.

Jake (*playing* **Rose**'s *dad*)   Okey-dokey, just me then.

Jake (*playing* **Rose**'s *dad*) *exits the reenactment area.*

Chloe (*playing* **Rose**'s *mum*)   Hang on, what are you saying? About sex?

Rose   We had sex OK, get over it!

Danny (*playing* **Joe**)   Rose –

Chloe (*playing* **Rose**'s *mum*)   I'm speaking to Rose actually, thank you, Joe.

Rose   Don't worry, Mum, it's all fine.

Chloe (*playing* **Rose**'s *mum*)   Is it? You used the contraceptives from the drawer?

Rose   No.

Chloe (*playing* **Rose**'s *mum*)   So, Joe brought some of his own?

Rose   No.

Chloe (*playing* **Rose**'s *mum*)   Then how on earth can you know that it is all fine? Did this really happen?

Rose   It did.

Danny (*playing* **Joe**)   Wait, Rose –

Chloe (*playing* **Rose**'s *mum*)   It's odd we haven't met you before, Joe, if you go to acting.

Danny (*playing* **Joe**)   I'm new to the group.

Chloe (*playing* **Rose**'s *mum*) *studies* **Danny** (*playing* **Joe**).

Chloe (*playing* **Rose**'s *mum*)   And you are a participant?

Danny (*playing* **Joe**)   Yes. Yyyyes. Yesssss I-I-I am.

Rose   Stop giving him the third degree, Mum. It's only sex.

Chloe (*playing* **Rose**'s *mum*)   I want you to think very carefully about what you are saying and whether or not it actually truthfully happened, Rose. I'm talking about when the penis and vagina connect.

Geoff   Stop right there!

Blossom   *Connect?*

Jake   Rose's mum has a very limited view of what counts as sex, as we are now all aware. Make of that what you will.

Rose   We. Had. Sex.

Jake   Typical Rose; a little white lie to take the drama to the maximum.

Blossom   Her mum deserves it. It's her fault for asking, when it is none of her business.

Chloe (*playing* **Rose**'s *mum*)   Definitely?

Rose   Yes!

Danny (*playing* **Joe**)   No! N-n-no.

Danny (*playing* **Joe**) *changes his physicality.*

Chloe (*playing* **Rose**'s *mum*)   David!

Rose (*loving the drama*)   Mum, please. This is so embarrassing.

Jake (*playing* **Rose**'s *dad*) *enters.*

Jake (*playing* **Rose**'s *dad*)   Everything OK?

Chloe (*playing* **Rose**'s *mum*)   Rose and Joe have had sex.

Jake (*playing* **Rose**'s *dad*)   Are you sure?

Rose   Actually, I prefer to say made love.

Danny (*playing* **Joe**)   N-n-no, R-r –

Danny   HANNAH MONTANA!

Chloe   Danny, what's up?

Danny   OK so yeah, am I allowed to do this?

Todd   Now he, now he asks us!

Blossom   Do what? I don't get it.

Danny *checks his arm.*

Danny   OK so yeah, Rose said Joe started to change his voice and stutter and I think. I mean, it seems like, you know . . .

Chloe   Joe was trying to look like a learning disabled person.

Danny   Yeah.

Rose   Oh, that's what he was doing. He did it so badly, though. He was a six out of ten at the most.

Chloe   Same as Danny, then.

Kev   Just be yourself, Danny! Be yourself! That is the best way!

Chloe   He can't be himself, Kev, because he's not learning disabled. Joe wasn't learning disabled.

Kev   What? *What?* He wasn't? Oh, wow! I thought he was! I really thought he was! Wow!

Todd   Danny, do you, do, do you need help?

Danny   OK so yeah, I do. Yes. I need help.

Jake   Correct answer. I'll be your coach.

Rose   I'll judge.

Kev   And me.

Blossom   Someone else should as well, you guys will love anything he does.

Todd   OK, OK I'll judge too.

Chloe   We don't have time for this. What about the police?

Todd   We can't we cannot let Danny humili humiliate himself in front of (*The audience.*) them.

Blossom   We can't, Chloe.

Geoff   No fair.

Chloe   Make it quick then.

Jake   First off, there's stimming. If you want to look learning disabled, you need to perfect your stimming. From what I've seen, yours is far from perfect.

Chloe   We don't all stim though.

Jake   That is true. You can choose pretty much anything as your stimming activity, as long as it's repetitive. It helps you when you want to daydream.

Todd   Or, or to concentrate, people use it for that too.

Jake   Yes. Daydreaming or concentrating. Come on then, choose your activity.

Danny   I'll do this.

Danny *shows them.*

Jake   No. Try tapping.

Todd   You could flap or spin.

Rose   Twiddle your hair.

Danny *does so.*

Rose   OK, that's better. I'd give that a ten.

Kev   Me too! Absolutely! Ten out of ten, Danny. Well done!

Todd   I'd, I'd give that a ten too.

Chloe   There's more to looking learning disabled than stimming. You could change your voice. There are different ways of doing a voice that sounds disabled so you'll need to find the one that suits you. You could try high?

Jake   Oooooh, listen to me and my high disabled voice.

Chloe   Or low, low and slow with lots of pauses.

Blossom   Or a stutter.

Rose   Do low.

Geoff (*low voice*)   I do believe there is a love train coming.

Chloe   So yeah anyway, choose your voice.

Danny (*doing a high and low voice*)   Could I do a mixture of high and low?

Blossom   Stick to what we are advising if you want to improve, Danny.

Danny   OK, how about this? Hi, my name is Joe, w-w-w-what's yours?

Kev   It's a ten from me, Danny. Fabulous!

Rose   I agree, five stars.

Jake   We are not doing stars actually, Rose.

Todd   It's not, it's not a ten from me. He sounds OK but not, not the thing he's saying.

Chloe   He should get himself an obsession. Danny, some people have obsessions, do you like anything?

Danny   Uh . . .

Blossom   Like *really* like it? For example, I love Only Fools and Horses. My favourite episode is 'The Jolly Boys' Outing' when they go on a beano to Margate. It first aired on Christmas Day 1989 and was the eighth year they did a Christmas special. But your interest could be anything.

Kev   Anything, Danny! Think! EastEnders! Neighbours!

Rose   From ten years ago. At least.

Jake   And you just jump straight in with it. Don't ask if they like Hannah Montana too, just say 'I like Hannah Montana'. You don't care whether they like it or not.

Kev   Buses! Trains! Tennis! Football!

Danny   I do like football.

Kev   Football! Yes, Danny! Football!

Blossom   Do you like talking about it?

Joe   Yeah, I think so.

Blossom   Then you have to talk about it.

Geoff   All. The. Time.

Kev   Go Danny! Go!

Danny   My favourite team is Spurs? Tottenham Hotspur. So. Spurs play football the right way, they're a club with ideals. Throughout their history, Spurs have had some incredible footballers who were brilliant entertainers: Ardiles, Gascoigne, Klinsmann, Ginola, Modric, Bale, van der Vaart. They were all great characters, mercurial and exciting. Spurs' motto is 'To dare is to do', which sort of encapsulates the club well.

We are a club who aspire to and try to reach the very highest level but we often fall short. We haven't won the league in sixty years nearly. But there's glory in the failure as the aspiration is admirable. To win, but to win the right way. Playing great football, with exciting players.

How was that?

Kev   You tried. You tried Danny, that's the main thing.

Rose   I'm sorry, Danny but that was terrible.

Chloe   You sounded like someone being interviewed.

Blossom   I didn't put it simply enough. You don't say *why* you like what you like. You need to list stuff. You need to say facts.

Kev   You did list the players, that was fantastic!

Chloe   Stay calm. Don't put emotion into it.

Jake   I know, learn from the master. The greatest showman. Todd, take the floor.

Geoff   Spotlight on Todd!

Todd *is given a spot.*

Todd   This is Liverpool Street. Change here for the Circle, Hammersmith and City and Metropolitan lines, and National Rail services. The next station is Bank.

There are beggars and buskers operating on this train, please do not encourage their presence by supporting them.

This is Bank. Please mind the gap between the train and the platform. Change here for the Circle, District, Northern and Waterloo and City lines, and the DLR. This is a Central line train to Ealing Broadway.

Much cheering and clapping.

Danny   I couldn't do that.

Jake   Do the states of America. Joe did the states of America.

Kev   He did! He did do that! Yes, yes he did.

Danny   America OK so yeah . . . Alabama, Texas, Minnesota, Idaho, Iowa, Georgia, Washington, Alaska . . . Illinois . . . Ohio . . . Kansas . . . uh

Blossom   Not like you're trying to remember, just say them.

Danny   Ohio, Virginia, Maryland, North Carolina, South Carolina, North Dakota, South Dakota, West Virginia, Mississippi, Wyoming, Oklahoma, Ohio, have I done that one? Utah, Indiana, Virginia . . . Rhode Island and Colorado!

Kev   Great obsession!

Rose   It's a ten from me, darling.

Todd   I, I give you, I give an eight. You missed you missed Hawaii.

Jake   And Florida and Montana and I don't think that was fifty so probably some others too. Impressive effort though Danny, I will say that.

Chloe   Now you just need to do things the right way.

Danny   Do things?

Kev   OK OK yeah, shake hands with everyone you meet! Shake hands in your own way! Make them feel welcome!

Jake   Freak out if someone touches you.

Todd   Or, hold their hand, give them a hug.

Chloe   Got it?

Rose   Do you understand, Danny?

Todd   Try to think differently. You've just got to think differently.

Danny   Think differently, yeah, good.

Chloe   So now, do everything you've learnt so far. All at once.

Kev   Danny, good luck! You got this!

Danny *stims. He says* –

Danny (*playing* **Joe**)   Hello, I'm Joe I'm Joe and I'm learning disabled.

Clapping and cheering.

Geoff   Boooom!

Kev   Three thousand per cent!

Rose   So much better than Joe!

Todd   You have passed. You have officially passed.

Chloe   Right, now Danny is not embarrassing himself can we please get on?

Danny   OK so yeah.

Rose   Let's go from when I said, 'Actually I prefer to say made love'. Actually I prefer to say made love.

Chloe (*playing* **Rose**'s *mum*; *to* **Rose**'s *dad*)   See? After all the chats we've had, Rose. Why didn't you talk to me about this?

Blossom   Who wants to talk to their mum about sex?

Todd   No thank you.

Kev   I would! I do, I do all the time!

Chloe (*playing* **Rose**'s *mum*)   I wouldn't have been angry.

Blossom   That doesn't mean she had to tell you, though!

Rose   I know you wouldn't.

Blossom   Can't anything be private?

Kev   No! Secrets are not good!

Blossom   But her mum doesn't have the right to know every thought in her head or to find out everything she does.

Kev   Mums worry, Blossom.

Blossom   That's their problem.

Chloe (*playing* **Rose**'s *mum*)   We could've just talked it through and made sure you were fully prepared. We trust you with a certain amount of freedom, you're even going to Margate in a few days –

Geoff   It's a free country.

Todd   Is, is it?

Geoff   Is it, indeed.

Blossom   On Tuesdays!

Chloe (*playing* **Rose**'s *mum*) – you need to trust us in return. Or have we been getting it all wrong? I don't know!

Kev Say sorry, Rose. Quick, your mum is sad!

Blossom And now the tears come out.

Rose You might want to know that Joe's penis doesn't work because of medicine he needs to take.

Danny/Danny (*playing* **Joe**) Oh my God.

Chloe (*playing* **Rose**'s *mum*) So you didn't have sex, then, truthfully?

Rose Truthfully we did, because we wanted to and the only reason we didn't is because we couldn't. So the real truth is we did, if you think about it.

Chloe (*playing* **Rose**'s *mum*) OK. OK, well that's good.

Rose Actually it's quite frustrating.

Jake (*playing* **Rose**'s *dad*) Joe, did you say we haven't met your family? (*To* **Chloe** (*playing* **Rose**'s *mum*).) Might be good to involve them too?

Danny (*playing* **Joe**) C-c-could we just . . .

Aaaah

Danny (*playing* **Joe**) *hugs* **Rose**'s *dad but somehow it goes wrong and it is weird and complicated.*

Geoff Ooof.

Todd What was that?

Danny (*playing* **Joe**) *goes to hug* **Rose**'s *mum.*

Rose Stop it!

Kev Yes, stop it!

Chloe (*playing* **Rose**'s *mum*) It's getting late, Joe you'll want to get home before it gets dark, won't you?

Rose   Stay, Joe.

Chloe (*playing* **Rose**'s *mum*)   It's pretty much YouTube time Rose, if you want me to get the laptop?

Rose   I know what you're doing.

Blossom   We all do.

Chloe (*playing* **Rose**'s *mum*)   Do you want EastEnders or are you more into Neighbours at the minute?

Rose   Don't try to distract me!

Jake (*playing* **Rose**'s *dad*)   Rose, I think Joe is taking advantage of you.

Kev   No! What?

Rose (*to her dad*)   How dare you!

Danny (*playing* **Joe**)   I-I-I'm not.

Jake (*playing* **Rose**'s *dad*)   I'm not sure he's who he says he is. You do sometimes misjudge situations.

Geoff   If truth be told.

Blossom   Not always though.

Geoff   Who to trust?!

Kev   Her parents! They love her, she's their baby!

Blossom   She's not a baby, she's a grown woman.

Geoff   They're older and wiser. They know the ropes.

Blossom   It's her right to have a boyfriend and be in love.

Geoff   It's risky behaviour. She's extremely vulnerable.

Blossom   Who says she's vulnerable?

Todd   If she doesn't take risks she can't learn.

Kev   Love is a risk! Love is always a risk!

Blossom   Exactly!

Rose   How dare you talk like that about my fiancé. Yes, it's true, we're getting married!

Danny (*playing* **Joe**)   N-n-n no, hang on.

Rose   Joe, just be yourself.

Jake (*playing* **Rose**'s *dad*)   Joe, I am asking you to leave. Right now!

Danny (*playing* **Joe**)   O-o-only if R-r-rose tells me to.

Kev   Leave, Joe, leave! You're upsetting people.

Blossom   No! Stay! She's not a kid. If they can't accept that, it's their problem not hers.

Danny (*playing* **Joe**)   I'll only leave if R-R-R-R-Rrose says I-I-I should.

Blossom *plays Susan Boyle 'I Dreamed a Dream' on the karaoke.*

Rose *sings the first three lines of the first verse of the song.*

Blossom   Actually, I've changed my mind. You should go.

Danny (*playing* **Joe**)   W-w-why?

Jake (*playing* **Rose**'s *dad*)   She's told you to leave, that should be enough. Let me show you the door.

Jake (*playing* **Rose**'s *dad*) *grabs* **Danny** (*playing* **Joe**) *and ushers him towards the door.*

Danny (*playing* **Joe**)   OK, OK, I'm g-going.

Rose's *dad forces* **Danny** (*playing* **Joe**) *out.*

Danny (*playing* **Joe**)   I'm gone.

Scene Ten

Projection: close-up on **Todd**, *The Past.*

Todd   I got these, I got these keys for you know, the you know you you know the pedalos. At the park. The pedalo shack. My job, you know my my my job to look after the pedalos at the park. Because they trust they do they do they trust me. And I trust you guys. There is an island, in the pond a, a, a, a duck island and I could take you there.

There is a woman in the cafe, you know near the park, near the gates, there's there's there's a woman there who serves who is the one who always comes to my table and she is my friend and we chat and she is my friend and we tell each other stuff and sometimes sometimes we joke, like banter, and then I say I say I have to go to my job now sorry I have to go to my job and she says 'Always busy, you'. And it is nice.

But yesterday wasn't wasn't like that, it wasn't like that. Because I couldn't drag the thoughts out of my, I didn't have any I didn't have any poetry just you know, just just you know humili humiliation and shame.

It was quiet because it was a cold a cold day yesterday so I took a pedalo I don't know why really I just wanted to not be not be near any people at all and and I I I went to the island and

You need to see for yourselves what it is like, that's what, that is what I am saying.

After after my shift I went back to the cafe and I ordered my white my white coffee normal milk one sugar and and and I ordered a waffle with maple syrup which I never do. That is unusual for me, I never do that. We chatted me and her and and I had banter and poetry and I was brilliant.

You could have that, you could have that too. You won't be disturbed on the island. You can recharge.

It could be ours. I trust you and they trust me so we need we need there does need to be rules

The rule the rules the rules for the island are we don't talk about the island and we don't bring anyone to the island. Those are those are the only two rules.

Scene Eleven

*The reenactment area is outside **Rose**'s house.*

Rose   Joe slept on the wall opposite my house all night, I saw him out of my bedroom window. So in the morning I called Todd to come and help in case he was still acting funny.

Blossom   *Why* did he do it? Why did he want to look like he was learning disabled?

Rose   It's obvious why: me. He was in love with me of course and wanted to keep seeing me.

Blossom   He didn't need to put on an act to keep seeing you. I bet it didn't even cross your mind whether he was learning disabled or not.

Rose   Of course it didn't, because I fall in love with the person. But look what happened with my parents.

Todd   I see, I do see what you are saying Rose. It was for the, you know the outside, the outside world. So he could keep hanging, hanging around with us.

Rose   With me.

Jake   Well, if Joe's attempt was anything like Danny's first one I really wouldn't blame one of you for putting him out of his misery. Let's get on with this then.

Rose   Do we have to? I'm so tired.

Danny   Me too.

Geoff   Me three.

Chloe   What do you need?

Geoff   A robe?

Stage management bring a martial arts robe onto stage.

Danny   A beer? Oh, regulations. A glass of water?

Rose Not you, Danny. I really need a break.

Danny OK so yeah, you can't talk to me like that. I passed, remember? I pass as you, so that means I get your privileges, right? So I can –

He stands behind a microphone.

Perfect height.
Look. I understand that I've got a job to do and I'm getting paid and –
but can I just –
because
I take issue with what Todd said a minute ago. I'm tired of hearing that shit on the Tube, let alone –

I know you were quoting, but there have been a few other comments that OK so yeah that have bothered me actually. I suppose I'm asking, because we are here on a stage and there's an audience – hi – I'm asking if we need to give space and time and a platform to an idea that shows such a lack of understanding of –

'Please do not encourage their presence by supporting them'

– a lack of understanding of –

I mean, what?! Even to my addled mind that doesn't make any sense. But worse than bad logic is the fact it ignores the root issue which is

the root issue is complicated but at the same time glaringly fucking obvious, glaringly glaringly—

Kev What is he saying?

Chloe Stop please, Danny. No swearing on stage. It's not your time to speak anyway.

Jake This is not all about you, remember.

Chloe If it's not on your arm, keep it in your head.

Danny   Maybe you think you can buy me but I'm not your pet.

Chloe *signals to stage management and a large hamster wheel appears.*

Chloe   On you get, Danny.

Danny   You're joking?

Chloe   I'm sorry because I think you probably do have some important things to say but we just don't have time for another normal's point of view, you know?

Geoff   Step on, my friend.

Danny   What? You know this is inhumane?

Todd   Is it, Danny? Do you think you might feel a bit on display? A bit like an exotic, abnormal, inferior monster?

Blossom   Todd means that's how one of us might have felt in Victorian times. We could have got put in a cage.

Geoff   Freak show.

Chloe   Will you get in the hamster wheel please Danny.

Danny   This is mad.

Blossom *puts Digital Underground 'Same Song', Justin Timberlake 'Love Stoned' and Fleetwood Mac 'Everywhere' on the karaoke.*

Blossom/Chloe/Geoff/Jake/Kev/Rose/Todd *sing the fifth and sixth lines of the first verse of 'Everywhere' by Fleetwood Mac.*

Danny   OK, OK.

Danny *gets onto the hamster wheel.* **Kev** *spins the wheel so that* **Danny** *has to run.*

Blossom/Chloe/Geoff/Jake/Kev/Rose/Todd *sing the first and second lines of the fifth verse of 'Same Song' by Digital Underground, the fourth line of 'Love Stoned' by Justin Timberlake and the chorus of 'Revolution' by Kirk Franklin.*

Chloe *and* **Kev** *take* **Danny** *out of the hamster wheel and into the reenactment area.* **Rose** *and* **Todd** *are already there.*

Chloe   It's the next morning now, Danny.

Danny (*playing* **Joe**)   Good morning. Where are you both off to?

Rose   You are doing your normal voice again.

Danny (*playing* **Joe**)   I don't need to do the other thing when it's just us.

Rose   Why?

Danny (*playing* **Joe**)   Montana, Florida, Alaska, Alabama, California . . .

Todd   Are you are you OK, Joe?

Danny (*playing* **Joe**)   I'm I'm I'm OK.

Rose (*to* **Todd**)   Told you. Weird.

Todd   Do you want to come to our island?

Danny (*playing* **Joe**)   Definitely.

Blossom *puts 'Everywhere' by Fleetwood Mac on the karaoke.*

Danny (*playing* **Joe**) *sings the second line of the chorus.*

Interval.

Act Two

Scene One

The reenactment area is a pond in Battersea Park.

Danny *runs slowly on the hamster wheel.*

Todd This announcement is for the normal people. You really need, you really need your wits about you. Because we are now on the island. And Joe died on the island. So the options of who killed him are narrowing and it is looking more and more like it could be one of us.

Jake Someone here is definitely getting locked up.

Todd I didn't think it would come to this. But guys, we are all going to have to prove ourselves. We are all on the suspects' list until we are taken off the suspects' list.

Danny *looks at his arm.*

Danny Rose. Rose and Todd. Let's move.

Rose Right, I need a shawl. I had my shawl on that morning. It's like Kate Winslet's in Titanic. Joe loved me in that shawl.

Kev *(calling to backstage)* A shawl, a shawl, we need a shawl for Rose.

Danny *(calling to backstage)* Come on, come on. They are all about to go down for murder.

A stage manager brings on a shawl.

Rose, **Todd** *and* **Danny** *(playing* **Joe***) enter the reenactment area on a pedalo.*

Rose *is on the back, her arms outstretched, the wind through her hair. Like Kate Winslet in Titanic.*

Danny *(playing* **Joe***)* I didn't know there was anything here.

Todd   There   isn't, there isn't anything.

Rose   Just us. That's the whole point of the island.

Danny (*playing* **Joe**)   I like the idea of that. Yeah, I love that. We can be free to think any way we want. We can be our true selves.

Jake   Our true murderer selves, does he mean? Is Joe predicting his own death here?

Geoff   A crime of passion? There is no Rose without a thorn.

Jake   Love does make people do crazy things.

Rose   HANNAH MONTANA! It was not me!

(*To* **Danny** (*playing* **Joe**).) Yes, Joe, you can be your true self on the island. You can see who you are.

Todd   You can you can see who someone else is.

Silence.

Danny   OK so yeah.

At school we had to design an island. It was an art project. The island of our dreams.

My island smelled like baking and sounded like waves against rocks. There were no houses. My bed was on top of the tallest tree. The thought of that island kept me going for years.

Rose   Joe didn't say all this.

Danny   He didn't. You never told me what you talked about on the pedalo so I made it up.

Chloe   I don't think he made that up.

Blossom   Me neither.

Chloe   I would've loved a bed in the trees too when I was a kid.

Geoff   Comfort and joy.

Rose   There would be no stairs on my island. Stairs are so repetitive.

They arrive at a small island.

Joe, we are here.

Rose *signals to* **Danny** (*playing* **Joe**) *and he helps her off the pedalo.*

Todd *ties the pedalo to a tree.* **Rose** *makes herself comfortable.*

Danny (*playing* **Joe**)   I can see why you love it here. No expectations. Freedom. It's magical.

Rose   You are being your self again.

Danny   I think it's the island. It lets me do that. Magical.

Rose   I don't think it's magical, Joe. But I do think it's the perfect place for a wedding.

Danny (*playing* **Joe**)   Have you always dreamed of getting married here?

Rose   No, but shall we?

Danny (*playing* **Joe**)   Yeah, yeah definitely. I'd love to.

Rose   OK.

Danny (*playing* **Joe**)   We need somebody to perform the ceremony.

Rose   Todd can do that. Todd's a very spiritual person.

Danny (*playing* **Joe**)   Amazing. Todd, do you think you could help us get married?

Todd   I can.

Rose *hands* **Danny** (*playing* **Joe**) *a stick.*

Rose   Joe, please write Joe hearts Rose in the earth.

He does so.

Rose   And a kiss.

He writes an X after their names.

Rose   Lovely.

Todd   Uh is there, is there anything that you want to say?

Danny (*playing* **Joe**)   Um . . .

Danny (*playing* **Joe**) *looks at his arm.*

Rose   Yes. I want to say. Joe. I love you. I want us to be one and not have any drama, arguments or cheating in the future.

Now you go.

Danny/Danny (*playing* **Joe**)   OK so yeah,
I want to feel the way you feel . . .
I want . . .
I just need. I need my.
HANNAH MONTANA! Sorry look, how much longer is this gonna take?
Cos I feel. And my man will be at stage door in twenty and he's come out of his way, you know?

Chloe   I don't think you should meet that man.

Danny   No well yeah probably but I am so. I think I know what happened to him, Joe.

Blossom   We didn't bring you here to think, Danny.

Danny   I'll do it a whole lot less once I get my hit.

Chloe   Are you OK, Danny? You look a bit sticky.

Danny   No, no, I'm cool.

Danny *yawns.*

Shall we get on?

Geoff   Once more with feeling.

Danny (*playing* **Joe**)   I want us to be one. I want to feel like you feel. And whilst I can't make any promises right now, yeah, the future.

Todd   With this uh, with this uh Joe, give me your lanyard please.

Danny (*playing* **Joe**) *hands* **Todd** *his lanyard.* **Todd** *looks at it, then puts it on* **Rose**.

Todd   With this lanyard, I thee wed.

Rose   Take our picture please, Todd.

Rose *hands* **Todd** *her phone. She and* **Danny** (*playing* **Joe**) *pose and* **Todd** *takes their photo.* **Rose** *looks at it.*

Rose   We look great. I'm sharing that.

Rose *sends a message.*

Todd   Now you have, you have your first dance if you want.

Rose   You know, getting married is very emotional for me. I need to get home for a rest. Let's go, husband.

Blossom *puts Rihanna 'Russian Roulette' on the karaoke.*

Danny (*playing* **Joe**) *sings the third line of the second verse, minus the first word.*

Todd   Come, come on, Joe. It will be dark soon.

Kev   But Joe stayed! In the dark! He loved that island!

Rose *wraps her shawl around* **Danny**.

Rose   See? We didn't kill him.

Jake   We know you didn't kill him at this point. We are looking for clues that you were the one who did it a few days later.

Chloe   There wasn't anything suspicious though, so we can take Todd and Rose off the list.

Jake   For now.

Scene Two

From this point onwards, the reenactment area is the island. **Danny** *is running on his hamster wheel.*

Kev   This is me! Yeah! Cos I saw the photo Rose sent from here and it looked fun. And I love fun! I do, I really love fun! I'm a fun, fun guy!

Danny *enters the reenactment area.*

Kev   Hey, hey!

Kev *enters the reenactment area.*

Danny (*playing* **Joe**)   Kev. Kev!

Kev   Yeah.

Danny (*playing* **Joe**)   Do you remember my name?

Kev   Joe!

Danny (*playing* **Joe**)   Yeah, yeah: Joe.

Kev   Joe Joe Joe Joe

Danny (*playing* **Joe**)   Joe, Joe, Joe, Joe –

*They jump up and down holding hands, laughing and saying '***Joe***' until they've no breath left,*

Kev/Joe   Joe Joe Joe Joe Joe Joe Joe Joe!

Danny (*playing* **Joe**)   I love this island.

Kev   Yeah!

Danny (*playing* **Joe**)   This is the life for us.

Kev   Yes, Joe! This is the life for us!

Danny (*playing* **Joe**)   Like Shipwrecked.

Kev   Like Shipwrecked, like Shipwrecked that's right, Joe!

Danny (*playing* **Joe**)   Like Robinson Crusoe! The Old Man and the Sea!

Kev   Love Island!

Danny (*playing* **Joe**)   Shutter Island!

Kev   Treasure Island!

Danny (*playing* **Joe**)   No man is an island!

Kev   Treasure island, Joe! There must be treasure here!

Danny (*playing* **Joe**)   Yeah! Yeah! Is that what you do, make stuff up, nothing's real here?

Kev   What do you mean, Joe?

Danny (*playing* **Joe**)   I don't know! I don't even know, Kev! There has to be treasure. Let's search.

Kev   OK, OK, OK, look.

Kev   Look look look look look: An X.

The kiss that **Joe** *scratched into the ground.*

Danny (*playing* **Joe**)   X marks the spot.

Kev   Omigod.

Danny (*playing* **Joe**)   Omigod.

Kev/Danny   Omigodomigodomigodomigodomi –

Kev   We're rich!

Danny (*playing* **Joe**)   What about –

Kev   Pirates!

Danny (*playing* **Joe**)   We should hide it.

Kev   Yeah.

Danny (*playing* **Joe**)   Where, where?

Kev   Think, think, think

Up the tree.

Danny (*playing* **Joe**)   Up the tree! Yes! Is there rope? There must be –

Kev   In the pedalo! There's! To tie the!

Kev *unties the rope from the pedalo.*

Danny (*playing* **Joe**)   Yeah, yeah great, so then we . . .

Kev   What do we do?

Danny (*playing* **Joe**)   Catapult it!

Kev   Yeah, we catapult it

Danny (*playing* **Joe**)   Up up up

Kev   The tree

Danny (*playing* **Joe**)   Up the tree. One.

Kev   Two

Danny (*playing* **Joe**)   Three

Kev   Up there.

Danny (*playing* **Joe**)   Yeah.

Kev   Yeah. Safe.

Danny (*playing* **Joe**)   Safe, / exactly.

Kev   Then I left. I left, because I had gardening club that afternoon.

Danny   OK so yeah.

Danny *gets back into his hamster wheel.*

Chloe   Well done, Kev. Joe looked so happy, he looked so happy there.

Blossom   He had more energy.

Chloe   This is probably when he started making that throne out of twigs.

Kev   So, did I do it, was it my fault?

Chloe   I think we can take you off the list at this point.

Jake   But we all know what Kev did, surely he is a suspect?

Chloe   Not right now though. Let's give him a bit of time of not being on there.

Scene Three

There is now a throne made from a tree stump and sticks on the island. **Danny** *(playing* **Joe***) is running on his hamster wheel.*

Jake   You must be getting tired, Danny, going round and round on there.

Geoff   A vicious circle.

Jake   Being tired is actually very useful, because I think I woke Joe up when I arrived onto the island.

Geoff   Neenaw neenaw, let's pick up the pace.

Danny   OK so yeah.

Danny *joins* **Jake** *in the reenactment area.*

Jake   Hello. You're here.

Danny *(playing* **Joe***)   Hello, friend.

Jake   Nobody stays here overnight.

Danny *(playing* **Joe***)   I slept. I slept well for the first time in ages.

Jake   Perhaps due to the excitement of yesterday. Rose sent us all a picture of the happy occasion.

Danny *(playing* **Joe***)   Yeah, maybe it was that. Or maybe the island.

Jake   When are you leaving, Joe? I came here to practice something.

HANNAH MONTANA! It just occurred to me that it is extremely interesting, isn't it, that Todd broke his own rule and brought Joe to the island? Perhaps it is him we should be looking at and not me. We definitely can't take him off the list of suspects yet.

Anyway, yes. When are you leaving the island, Joe?

Danny (*playing* **Joe**)   I'm not sure I will leave.

Jake   That is not very convenient for me. Although yes, maybe it actually means I don't need to practice because you can just do this for me.

Danny (*playing* **Joe**)   Can you explain, Jake?

Jake   I'm supposed to be signing on tomorrow.

Danny (*playing* **Joe**)   OK.

Jake   But I need to get out of it. If I don't have a break from those patronising bastards this week I don't know what will happen.

Danny (*playing* **Joe**)   I hear you. Sometimes you just need to escape. That's why we need the island, right?

Jake   Yes, I have to get two buses to the job centre and they are very strict on all their appointment timings and the thing about buses is, I always get distracted and miss the stop and turn up half an hour late. And if I'm not half an hour late, I'm three hours early and if they finally agree to see me anyway, nothing my work coach says makes sense and it's incredibly painful. That's the reason I need you to be Karl Kennedy.

Danny (*playing* **Joe**)   Who's Karl Kennedy?

Jake   The artistic director of our acting group. You'll do him better than me. You should say there's something going on that I can't miss so I won't be able to sign on tomorrow.

Danny (*playing* **Joe**)   Right.

Jake   Just don't tell them I'll actually be taking in some sea air in Margate then singing my lungs out in a karaoke bar. This is my work coach's direct line.

Jake *passes* **Danny** (*playing* **Joe**) *his phone.*

Jake   He's not the warmest character. I'm pretty sure he takes the piss out of me the minute I'm out the door. 'My name's Jake James and I can't even speak properly never mind do a job.' That's what he says to them all, I imagine.

Danny (*playing* **Joe**)   I'll call now shall I?

Jake   Yes.

Danny (*playing* **Joe**) *makes the call.*

Geoff (*playing* **Des**)   Hello?

Danny (*playing* **Joe**)   Hello, is this Des?

Geoff (*playing* **Des**)   JSA2.6

Todd   That is, that is exactly how they sound, Geoff.

Kev   Yes Geoff! So good!

Danny (*playing* **Joe**)   Hello Des, JSA2.6 Jake James.

Geoff (*playing* **Des**)   JABS.

N/ENT.

Danny (*playing* **Joe**)   MA?

Geoff (*playing* **Des**)   N/ENT, NFA.

Jake   What's going on? Is it working?

Danny (*playing* **Joe**)   MOP. WCA.

Geoff *sighs. Hold music.*

Danny (*playing* **Joe**, *to* **Jake**)   I'm on hold. You're right, he's an idiot. He's getting theI I told him to get his manager. manager.

Blossom *plays* **Angie**, *the manager.*

Blossom (*playing* **Angie**)   LCW?

Danny (*playing* **Joe**)   Ah, MPB MA, Angie.

Blossom (*playing* **Angie**) *laughs.*

Blossom (*playing* **Angie**)   ES5JP?

Danny (*playing* **Joe**)   DWP NSESAF1 ESA.

Blossom (*playing* **Angie**)   NSESAF1?

Danny (*playing* **Joe**)   NSESAF1.

Blossom (*playing* **Angie**)   . . . LA . . . DWP, WCA, UC50.

Danny (*playing* **Joe**, *to* **Jake**)   All done.

Jake   What? Is that what she said?

Danny (*playing* **Joe**)   No signing on for six weeks.

Jake   Six weeks?

Danny (*playing* **Joe**)   That's what I requested and that's
what she gave us.

Jake   Well I'm glad I asked you to be Karl Kennedy, I must
say.

Danny (*playing* **Joe**)   It gets better, listen to this. (*Into phone.*)
There's one more thing, Angie. Your colleague, the man
who usually handles Jake's account?

Blossom (*playing* **Angie**)   Des?

Danny (*playing* **Joe**)   Des, that's it. I'd like to make a
complaint about him. You see, he mimicked Jake last week as
he left the room.

Jake   No, no. That's what I *imagined* he did.

Danny (*playing* **Joe**)   It's completely unacceptable. He
should be the one seeking new employment, in my opinion.
He cannot get away with imitating Jake.

Jake   Can you stop it, that's, that's not what happened.

Blossom (*playing* **Angie**)   I'm going to look into this, leave it with me.

Danny (*playing* **Joe**)   Thanks so much, Angie.

Blossom *puts The Notorious B.I.G. on the karaoke.*

Danny (*playing* **Joe**) *sings the first five lines and the chorus from 'The Sky's the Limit' by The Notorious B.I.G.*

Danny (*playing* **Joe**)   Six weeks of freedom!

Jake   I don't think you should've said that about Des. I don't want to get someone sacked.

Danny (*playing* **Joe**)   But he is a horrible person.

Jake   He might be. He might be a horrible person, Joe. But I might be paranoid, I might be letting my imagination run away with me in an unhelpful way. The point is, Joe, I didn't want you to do that.

Danny (*playing* **Joe**) *doubles over for a moment in pain. Then he is back up.*

Danny (*playing* **Joe**)   Alabama, Alaska, Arizona – I can do them in alphabetical order now, look – Arkansas, California, Colorado – (*To* **Jake**.) OK so yeah, he just kept going and going you said? –

Jake   Yes, it got very boring so I went home.

Danny *sits on the hamster wheel.*

Blossom   When I first moved into assisted housing, a woman said she wanted to use my toilet but when I let her in, she actually stole my laptop. I felt so ashamed I hid from everyone and lived off bread and jam for three months until I could afford to get a new one from Cash Converters.

Chloe   Oh, that's what was going on with you!

Blossom   I'm just saying, I can see what Joe is doing here. He's avoiding. He doesn't want to hear what Jake is telling him.

Jake   He did go on for a very long time.

Blossom   Bet it didn't feel very good to have all Joe's words running rings around you Jake, cos that is when you sent the WhatsApp saying Joe is shifty.

Danny *gets back into his hamster wheel. Perhaps he sits this time.*

Jake   Yes, that is right, Blossom. That was very unsettling if you know what I mean.

Blossom   Yeah, I'd be unsettled too if I got somebody the sack.

Jake   I did not get Des the sack, that was Joe, getting high on power, the arrogant, articulate show-off. Ah ha. Yes, I see what you are doing, Blossom. Very clever. You are trying to make me sound like I am the murderer. But I didn't do it, so you can take me off the list.

Blossom   I think we should keep you on there as we have now discovered you have a motive.

Jake   Take me off the list.

Blossom   But you are literally the only one of us so far with a motive.

Chloe   Try to trust in the plan, Jake.

Jake   I am being set up here.

Scene Four

Danny *sits in his hamster wheel.*

Kev   This was when, this was when

Because Jake said don't trust him, in the WhatsApp, and so I thought, why not –

Why not go and see, but I was wrong because he, this is when he, this is when –

I don't know if I can do this.

Danny   You can, Kev. I know you can.

Danny *enters the reenactment area.*

Danny (*playing* **Joe**)   Hey, hey Kev!

Kev   Joe, Joe. Hey Joe, can I trust you, Joe?

Danny (*playing* **Joe**)   Course you can, Kev, it's me, Joe.

Kev   Cos Jake thinks: no! He could be wrong though, he could be wrong!

Danny (*playing* **Joe**)   Exactly, because it's me, Joe.

Kev   Joe! I trust you, Joe!

Danny (*playing* **Joe**)   Yes, Kev!

Kev   Yes, Joe!

Kev/Danny   Yessssss!

Kev *sees* **Rose**'s *shawl and* **Joe**'s *shoes.*

Kev   Oh.

Danny (*playing* **Joe**)   Shall we dig for treasure, Kev?

Kev   Oh, you're.

Danny (*playing* **Joe**)   And catapult! Up the trees, again?

Kev   You're you're you're sleeping here?

Danny (*playing* **Joe**)   Yeah.

Kev   But – all night?

Danny (*playing* **Joe**)   Yeah.

Kev   Yeah, yeah, yeah – Why?

Danny (*playing* **Joe**)   Treasure, Kev! Then we'll catapult! Remember?

Kev   But you should sleep at home.

Danny (*playing* **Joe**)   At home, yeah.

Kev   Have you got family?

Danny (*playing* **Joe**)   Yeah, yeah my mum.

Kev   Your mum, she'll be. You should call her, see her –

Danny (*playing* **Joe**)   Yeah OK OK see her.

Blossom *plays Anne Marle 'Perfect to Me' on the karaoke.*

Kev   She'll be sick with worry.

Danny (*playing* **Joe**)   Yeah, yeah, maybe.

Danny (*playing* **Joe**) *sings the bridge.*

Kev   You can't stay here.

Danny (*playing* **Joe**)   It's Treasure Island though! Love Island!

Kev   She'll be – won't she? – sick with worry.

Danny (*playing* **Joe**)   No, don't think so.

Kev   But Joe! Mums! They – sick with worry and and and you're her baby and what if she thinks
if if if if if
she
what if
what what what –

Danny/Danny (*playing* **Joe**) *doubles over in pain. He stands.*

Danny (*playing* **Joe**)   You can go and see her. Tell her I'm fine.

Kev   OK, OK, Joe.

Danny (*playing* **Joe**)   You can. Great. Sorted.

Kev   But! I don't know where she lives! I might not say it right!

Danny (*playing* **Joe**)   I'll write her a letter. I'll tell you the address. You can give her a letter.

Kev   Yes, yes tell her you are on the island, this island. I can do this! Yes! I've got this! Write it, Joe!

Danny (*playing* **Joe**)   Later!

Kev   Write it now, Joe! (*To* **Danny**.) That's when you, go on, go on.

Kev *hands* **Danny** *a piece of paper and pen.*

Kev   HANNAH MONTANA! See, see, I thought it was fun for Joe to do this trick. But no. Uh-uh. I don't think he wanted to but he had no choice because I kept going on and on about his mum. Me, I wouldn't hurt a fly but if someone says something that really really makes me, you know, scrambles my brain, I sometimes accidentally, you know

Kev *mimes throwing a punch.*

Just to make them stop saying it. It's like that. (*To* **Danny**.) Keep going.

Danny (*playing* **Joe**) *writes.*

Danny (*playing* **Joe**)   Wyoming, Vermont, Vermont. Montana, Indiana, Georgia!

Kev   What? Will she understand?

Danny (*playing* **Joe**) *continues writing.*

Danny (*playing* **Joe**)   She'll understand yeah yeah yeah. New York. Georgia. Arizona. Alabama, Joe.

Kev   Will she know what that means? Are you sure?

Danny (*playing* **Joe**)   Yep yep, yeah yeah yeah.

Kev   Yeah?

Danny (*playing* **Joe**)   Yeah.

It says how I'm on Treasure Island and X marked the spot and

Kev   We're rich!

Danny (*playing* **Joe**)   We're rich! We found treasure and

Kev   And and you're happy!

Danny (*playing* **Joe**)   Yeah.

Kev   You love it here!

Danny (*playing* **Joe**)   Yeah.

Kev   And you are OK.

Danny (*playing* **Joe**)   Yeah, yeah.

Kev   You are on the island and it is all good!

Kev   This is when I went to Crystal Palace and saw his mum and and and, you know.

Jake   Returned to the island and killed Joe?

Kev   I didn't do it. I don't think I did it.

Todd   Sorry, Kev, sorry but we do we do have to put you back on the suspects' list.

Scene Five

Chloe *brings* **Danny** *to the forestage and hands him a glass of water. She returns to her spot in the puzzler area. Projection of a hand-written note which reads: close-up of* **Danny**. *The Past.*

Danny *is bathed in golden light. He lies down and looks up at the clouds. He's happy.*

Danny   You're here. Lie down. This is the spot. This is the spot. Lie.

See here, a dragon? See it? That bit's its wings, then it's legs are sort of. Galloping. If you look through the – no, no it's moving now, it's changing, it's turning into, into something else.

Shame. That was a good one.

Got refreshments. Diet Coke. Couple of Boost bars. Water.

OK so yeah: man walks into a shop and peruses the confectionary shelves – do you know this one? – so he walks into the shop, makes his pick, goes up to the counter and says 'I'll have a Twirl, a Boost and a Whispa' and the cashier goes

Danny *spins round. Points and whispers.*

You're amazing!

He laughs.

Last night was. Gonna have a few days off it? Maybe a month. Maybe save it for weekends only, see what happens.

This weather. Relaxes your very bones.

Could stay here all day.

Yeah,

this is Heaven.

Scene Six

Danny *walks on the hamster wheel while* **Jake** *tries to look at his arm.*

Jake   Yes. Right. Next up should be Chloe and Blossom. We need to do when they are on the pedalo on their way to see Joe.

Chloe   But Joe wasn't on the pedalo.

Jake   I think it is important to see. Because I heard you describe this bit to Danny in the van and it sounded fascinating, if not a bit violent and incriminating.

Blossom   It will be a waste of time though.

Chloe   Aren't you worried about the police, Jake?

Jake   It is the police I am doing this for. We are on yesterday, the day Joe died. So excuse me if I find it a bit suspicious that you told Danny that you made a plan on the pedalo.

Chloe   We didn't do anything wrong.

Blossom   We kind of did a bit, Chloe.

Chloe   Alright. Fair enough, Jake. But just for the record, I don't feel ashamed of what you're about to see. Let's do this, Blossom.

Blossom *and* **Chloe** *get into the pedalo.* **Blossom** *pedals fast.*

Blossom   Why on earth would Kev go to see Joe when Jake has said he is shifty?

Chloe   It doesn't make any sense.

Blossom   He will probably end up marrying Joe or something, like Rose did.

Kev   I didn't though! I didn't!

Chloe   I really hope Kev is alright. It's not like him not to reply to messages for a whole day.

Kev   Sorry guys, I'm, I'm so sorry. I was busy! Yeah, I was lost in Crystal Palace!

Blossom   A bit of help would be good, Chloe.

Chloe   I don't think I can see him, Joe.

Blossom   We can go back if you like?

Chloe   We need to make sure Kev is OK.

Danny *curls up in the hamster wheel.*

Blossom   Also, you have got unfinished business.

Jake   Aha!

Geoff   The plot thickens.

Chloe   What do you mean?

Blossom   You told me that you didn't say to Joe what you wanted to, at acting.

Chloe   I'm sorry, Blossom. I'm really sorry. You were the first to see that he wasn't right and I sent you out of the room.

Blossom   It's OK.

Chloe   It's not. I knew too, deep down, cos of how he made me feel.

Blossom   We all make mistakes. Don't blame yourself.

Chloe   I should have done something. I should've confronted him.

Blossom   You can now.

Chloe   I don't think I can look at him let alone speak to him.

Blossom   You need to do this, Chloe. I'm with you. We'll do this for all of us. He won't leave our island, he upset Jake, God knows what he's done to Kev, he tried to get inside my head and he stole your sentences.

Chloe   But he'll say he can't understand me. It will be like when people say I'm too slow, I'm like a child, I'm not responsible. Then he will talk fast and say long words and they will come quick and they will be the right words.

Blossom   I know how you feel. But it's OK. You can use all those people who have said you are slow. You can take your revenge on them now.

Jake   Did you all get that? Revenge.

Geoff   Don't get mad, get even.

Blossom   Imagine he's that teacher at secondary. Or the man behind you in the queue at the Post Office or Paul Robinson from my Year Nine class or, or

Chloe   Or that doctor to my mum when I was born.

Blossom   Exactly. All men?

Chloe   Uh huh.

They consider.

He'll say we're wrong.

What if we are wrong?

Blossom   Whatever he says and however he twists things, the words to remember are *fucking tourist cunt.*

Chloe   Blossom, you never speak like that.

Blossom   Call him a fucking tourist cunt because he is a fucking tourist cunt. We are not wrong.

Chloe   We are not wrong.

Blossom (*to backstage*)   We need thunder, please. We need lightning.

Stage management brings thunder and lightning.

Blossom *roars.* **Chloe** *roars. Rain crashes down around them. They pedal furiously.*

Kev   Go Chloe, go Blossom!

Jake   Yes, I do agree, I do agree with Kev actually. I still think there is a high chance you might have killed Joe and I am not sure he absolutely entirely deserves it but I do I do actually support you both, yes. You are definitely still on the suspects' list though. In fact, you've got straight to the top of it, in my opinion.

Chloe   I think next has to be me and Blossom on the island? Are we next, Danny?

Everyone turns to **Danny** *who is asleep in the hamster wheel.*

Geoff   Asleep on the job. Wake up sleepy head.

Chloe *checks* **Danny**'s *arm.*

Chloe   It's me and Blossom on the island. His skin feels weird, cold and sweaty.

Jake   Sorry, Chloe, but Danny is not fit to do this job.

Geoff   Out for the count. Drug sick.

Todd   I can, I can be Joe.

Chloe   Great idea, Todd.

Todd *reads* **Danny***'s arm. He does a double take and looks closer.*

Todd   Just give me two, give me two minutes.

Kev   You got this, Todd! Good luck! You got this!

Scene Seven

Projection of a handwritten note which reads: close-up on **Kev***. The Past.*

Kev   Hi Mum, hi

Oh voicemail good cos you might say

No! Don't go! Ha, that rhymes.

whoooosh!

did you hear that?

I'm at the station, on the bridge

sorry

I've been having those thoughts again.

I'm

up high,

watching people which is a bad idea because

jealousy! enviously!

they're busy with places to go and I want places to go to like

university

Ibiza

and I want to have

a

job

and a

car and

sex

and I'm tired of spreading love and giving out

hugs and lighting up the room with my smile

because life is full of

joy and

wonder.

I'm tired of not having those thoughts not having those
thoughts not having those thoughts

So

I have been having those thoughts

again

I'm deep deep down.

I was in my room and you know how my brain goes? My
brain pushed me

downhill!

all the way downhill and I wanted to get up to go uphill but
it pushed me down all the time so I say

Kev, you need a a a

a plan!

Whooooosh! Ha!

In the future one day you'll die Mum sorry, and Dad too and that's

sad!

and I'll go into a home and be looked after by people who

don't care!

and be all alone really alone and that's the

future

so, yeah yeah I'm a bit sad

I'm having those thoughts again sorry

I'm deep deep down

drowning.

But I have worked out a plan and and and the plan is

– drumroll, ta daaaa –

Jump!

Go first

Die Mum, that's what I'm saying.

But then you'll be sad, Dad'll be sad

So

Should I? I don't know. What should I do?

you can tell me when you hear this

When will you hear this?

I'll wait till you tell me what to do. I think I can wait

come quick

can you come quick

What shall I do?

Scene Eight

Todd (*playing* **Joe**) *is in the reenactment area. Soaked.*

Todd (*playing* **Joe**)   Wyoming, West Virginia, Wisconsin, Washington, Virginia, Vermont, Utah, Texas, Tennessee, South Dakota, South Carolina, Rhode Island –

Chloe   Joe! Joe!

Blossom   Hey Joe!

Todd (*playing* **Joe**) *stops.*

Todd (*playing* **Joe**)   Oh. Hello. Welcome to my island. How can I help you?

Blossom   Where is Kev?

Todd (*playing* **Joe**)   Kev?

Chloe   Yeah, Kev. He said on WhatsApp he was coming here but now he's not replying.

Todd (*playing* **Joe**)   He did! Kev! So fun!

Blossom   Where is he, Joe?

Chloe   We're worried about him.

Todd (*playing* **Joe**)   No! Don't worry about Kev. Kev's fine. He's doing me a favour.

Chloe   What favour?

Todd (*playing* **Joe**)   Well, doing himself a favour really. He's gone to my mum's. He's putting his mind at ease. Maybe he'll put my mum's mind at ease too. Maybe he'll be the son she always wanted.

Chloe   I don't think this sounds like a very good idea. Kev might get lost.

Todd (*playing* **Joe**)   What, no, it's fine.

Blossom   Where does your mum live?

Todd (*playing* **Joe**)   We're on my island and it's all good here. I love this place. Can I have a hug?

Chloe   Are you OK, Joe?

Blossom   He wants a hug, Chloe.

Chloe   Oh yeah. Alright.

As **Chloe** *and* **Todd** (*playing* **Joe**) *hug,* **Blossom** *ties the rope from the pedalo around* **Todd** (*playing* **Joe**)*, his arms are bound behind him.*

Todd (*playing* **Joe**)   What – is this another wedding ritual?

Chloe *and* **Blossom** *force* **Todd** (*playing* **Joe**) *to sit down.*

Chloe   You're angry. You come here to get angry? To vent?

Blossom   Yes.

Blossom *gags* **Todd** (*playing* **Joe**).

Blossom   You are going to listen to us now. We will make you listen to us. Why isn't my freedom pass valid in commuter hours, don't you expect me to ever get a job? I am not surplus to requirements. I don't want to just sit in front of the TV or YouTube or my bedroom window.

Chloe   Yes, Blossom! That was brilliant.

Blossom   Your go. You can do it, Chloe!

Chloe   Hey, hey you! Yes, you. You just need to wait for a minute. Have you really got such important things to do? Are you really in such a hurry that you can't wait for me to find my words? Well, you're missing out if you don't sort that out and your small print format and your stairs and and and and how bad at being flexible you are. Because you are so bad at being flexible. There is no give in you at all.

Blossom   You can't pick and choose. Listen: I'm not a fancy-dress costume you get to take on and off. I am me. All the time.

Todd (*playing* **Joe**) *takes off his gag.*

Chloe   You, you fucking t–

Todd (*playing* **Joe**)   Look. Alphabetical, backwards! Wyoming, Wisconsin, West Virginia Washington –

Blossom *goes to* **Todd** (*playing* **Joe**).

Blossom   Quick, help me tie him up again.

Todd (*playing* **Joe**)   You didn't tie me. You don't do knots properly.

He shakes the ropes off.

Can I not I pick and choose? You are choosing to blame me for things I didn't even do, like I'm the same as all the rest, even though you know there is no rest and that we all think differently. But if that's what you do here, fine. I can do that. I can do that, I can do that to you. I can make you all the people to blame in my life. (*To* **Blossom**.) Sit down.

Blossom   No.

Todd (*playing* **Joe**)   Sit down. Or we could do what you both did to me, hug and then I force you to sit down?

Blossom   It's fine.

Blossom *sits.*

Todd (*playing* **Joe**)   Now you, Chloe.

Chloe   I don't want to.

Todd (*playing* **Joe**)   Come on, it's just like you did to me. I'll untie you once I've finished. You were going to untie me, right?

Chloe   Yeah.

Todd (*playing* **Joe**)   Great. Go on, then. Sit. Come on, it's not fair otherwise.

Chloe *sits down.* **Todd** (*playing* **Joe**) *binds* **Chloe**'s *and* **Blossom**'s *wrists and ankles. He gags their mouths.*

Todd (*playing* **Joe**)   OK, OK, OK, so you you you

Todd (*playing* **Joe**) *doubles over in pain. He stands.*

(*To* **Blossom**.) Mum. Your expectation and disappointment and concern weigh so heavy on me. I can't do anything except fail, but the offer of your spare room and alarm clock and appointments diary never let me even do that properly.

(*To* **Chloe**.) Agatha. You killed my one passion. My passion was the why and the how, but you said, forget that if you want to get them through. If you don't want to let them down, you said, focus on the dates, teach to the test. Don't ignite a fire in them for god's sake, get them to pass. So now I'm tired of the sound of my own voice and tired of the faces looking up at me thinking I know what I'm talking about when in fact I am a fraud and if I know one thing it is that the bright future they're expecting doesn't exist.

Jasmine. You told me open up, confide, don't be such a man. You regret it when people are over though, don't you? When I'm too much and selfish and weird. Deny it all you like, but I know you are thinking about lengths of leases and clocks ticking when I can't even, I can't think past, past-

When I am tired of the sound of my own thoughts.

Geoff   Joe tried to do the same as Blossom and Chloe to no avail. What made them strong as steel made him weak as water.

Todd (*playing* **Joe**)   I think that's all I've got. So you just say it and then . . . feel . . .?

Should I untie you now?

Blossom *and* **Chloe** *nod.* **Todd** (*playing* **Joe**) *unties them throughout the following.*

Todd (*playing* **Joe**)   You're not scared, are you? All I want to do is think like you, so I don't have to think like me. You acted like it was a crime, Blossom. But it was that or. It's life or death for me, you see. So, I don't think it's that bad. I don't. I don't. I'm just trying to work something out. I thought you guys could help me but you can't. I'm beyond help I think. I'm the problem, it's too deep within me.

Kev *enters.*

Kev   Joe, Joe, Joe.
I found, I found, I
hoped it would be the right door and
I'm a friend!
and,
I'm a friend!
I don't know you but
I've got your son!
I've, no
your son is on
Treasure Island!
and
X marks the spot
It is it is

OK, OK

OK

Just read the, read the –
Here
here here

I, I can't
I can't read it
because
Because because
I can't

Well I don't lie, so
I'm a nice person
I'm helping
I am I'm –
Read it

Pause.

See. See?

Pause.

See?

Why are you
Yes! Yes, his writing! I know! I know!
Don't
I'm a good person
Don't cry

To **Todd** (*playing* **Joe**).

You made me –
I am a good person
She cried
she shouted
'out, out'
You made me
make her,
I'm a nice person
and
she *cried*

I am a good person

Kev *hits* **Todd** *(playing* **Joe***).* **Todd** *(playing* **Joe***)'s gag falls off.*

Kev   I never make people cry. I don't, I
she didn't *understand*
she didn't know what it *meant*
Treasure Island because she said –
No! Um hang on,
She said, for you
She said a a a a
appointment!
A dentist appointment! That's it!

Todd *(playing* **Joe***)*   What?

Kev   It was two days ago, Joe! You missed it!

Jake, **Rose** *and* **Geoff** *enter on a pedalo.*

Jake   What's going on here? And why is no one answering
their WhatsApps?

Kev   She booked. For the dentist!

Todd *(playing* **Joe***)*   I don't need her to. I'm a grown
I'm a
man

Kev   You missed it! She cried! People from work are calling,
she said! She doesn't know what to do!

Todd *(playing* **Joe***)*   Fucksake

Kev   She cried Joe. You made me make her cry because she
couldn't read the letter! You forgot your appointment!
People are calling!

Todd *(playing* **Joe***)*   Jesus. Can you.

(To **Kev***.)* I don't need her appointments, you retard.

Kev *hits* **Todd** *(playing* **Joe***). He's out cold.*

Rose   You brute! This marriage is over!

Jake Shit.

Blossom Kev!

Kev Oh no, oh no!

Blossom (*to* **Joe**) This is not your island, it's ours. You're not even using it right. It's somewhere to scream, not somewhere to live. It's not somewhere to hide away, it's somewhere to help you go back out into the world. We don't want to be separate.

Chloe You fucking tourist cunt!

Geoff *What?* Sensei Geoff is losing the plot.

Jake Chloe, you've done first aid, what should we do?

Chloe We should, we should call an ambulance.

Jake Police come with an ambulance.

They all look at **Kev**.

Kev Oh god oh god oh god.

Then, over the PA system,

Stage Door Keeper Mr Danny Taggart to stage door. Mr Danny Taggart to stage door please, you have a visitor.

Blossom Danny, I think that's your drug dealer.

Geoff It's payday.

Jake Is he trying to live here?

Danny *sits bolt upright.*

Danny What's going on?

Jake You are back with us, Danny. You haven't missed much.

Kev I killed Joe! Did you see that? It was me! It was me! This is bad! This is so, so bad!

Chloe He still has a pulse, but it's not looking good.

Danny   You haven't got to the end yet?

Chloe   Not yet.

Danny   OK so yeah, you need to get to the end.

Todd   We do because Kev didn't kill him.

Kev   So. No. OK. OK! Todd! I believe you.

Danny   Shall we get this done then?

Chloe   Where were we? Yeah, Kev said Oh God oh God.

Kev   Oh God oh God oh God!

Blossom   Joe's OK. We don't need to call an ambulance because he's OK. Can we just go Margate, Rose's mum is waiting in the van at the gate.

Jake   Let's go.

Blossom, **Geoff**, **Jake** and **Kev** *go to the pedalos.* **Rose** *and* **Chloe** *linger.*

Chloe   You know, I'm gonna leave my phone with him. Just in case.

Chloe pushes her phone into **Danny** *(playing* **Joe***)'s pocket.*

Chloe   Plenty more fish in the sea, Rose.

Rose   Yeah.

Chloe   I think you should choose the songs tonight, Rose. First up Beastie Boys?

Scene Nine

Projection of a handwritten note which reads: close-up on karaoke in Margate. Yesterday 2pm.

Blossom, **Chloe**, **Geoff**, **Jake**, **Kev**, **Rose** *and* **Todd** *sing the chorus of 'Fight for Your Right to Party' by the Beastie Boys.*

Scene Ten

Continues from Scene Seven.

Geoff No time to lose. What's next for Joe?

Todd (*playing* **Joe**) *sits up. He gets up.*

Kev So what did Joe do? What did he do?

Todd (*playing* **Joe**) Indiana, Arizona, Alabama, Alaska, Florida . . . Think differently. Just think differently.

Minnesota, North North Dakota, South Dakota, Louisiana . . .

Oklahoma.

Kev It's not working. He is deep deep down.

Danny This has got to be rock bottom. What he was chasing doesn't work. He's got no options left.

Blossom *puts Lead Belly 'Good Morning Blues' on the karaoke.*

The first two lines of the chorus are visible on the screen, but all is silent.

Todd (*playing* **Joe**) *looks out across the pond.*

Todd I think he walked, he walked into the water and drowned himself.

Todd *strides purposely into the water.*

A phone rings.

Todd (*playing* **Joe**) What?

Todd (*playing* **Joe**) *stops walking.*

Geoff Joe stopped dead in his tracks.

Jake He didn't know a phone was there. Chloe put it in his pocket.

Kev It was a surprise.

Chloe   He reached for the phone.

Todd (*playing* **Joe**) *moves to take the phone out of his pocket –*

Rose   With his left hand, Joe was left handed.

Todd (*playing* **Joe**) *switches hands and takes the phone from his pocket. He keeps walking.*

Chloe   He looked at the screen.

Todd (*playing* **Joe**) *looks at the screen.*

Todd   Blossom?

Blossom   He rejected the call.

Todd (*playing* **Joe**) *rejects the call.*

Blossom   Yeah, I did call him at some point but he rejected the call. It was early this morning. Just after it got light. I felt bad about how we left him, even after everything. He had no way off the island.

Todd *puts the phone in his pocket. He keeps walking.*

Kev   No! He rejected the call. He didn't ignore it! He you know you know! Stopped! It stopped his thoughts for a second! He went back to the island. Go back to the island, Todd.

Todd (*playing* **Joe**) *returns to the island. He sits down on the shore.*

Todd   Then he didn't, I don't think he did it because the, the wild swimmers come at 6am and it starts to get busy.

Chloe   Let's see what time Blossom called.

Chloe *takes her phone from* **Todd**.

Chloe   5.34 a.m. Wait. There's another number on here. An outgoing call was made right after. It lasted an hour and forty-six minutes. I'm gonna call it.

Kev   No! Chloe! It might be a scam!

Chloe *dials the number and puts her phone on speaker. A ring tone and then, 'Hello, you've reached Samaritans,' and another ring tone.*

Chloe *hangs up.*

Chloe   He's OK. He didn't do it. He is OK for now.

Geoff   Washed up, on the shore.

Todd   Why was his shoe in the water if he didn't drown?

Kev   But, his shoe was in the water!

Chloe   He must've taken his shoes off to swim across the pond. We got it wrong. He didn't drown and nobody killed him. We misread the signs.

Jake   If there is no victim then the police cannot be after us.

Kev   But we saw them at the park, right across from the island.

Geoff   Neenaw neenaw.

Kev   So loud.

Blossom   They could've been there for the kids smoking weed by the pavilion.

Todd   But, but we, we were in a car chase.

Blossom   I didn't actually see a car behind us though. Did anyone else?

Chloe   Then why did Rose's mum drive so fast?

Rose   My mum loves a drama. It was probably all in her head.

Todd   We saw them when we picked up Danny, we saw them then.

Danny   OK so yeah, police go down Victoria Street all the time.

Chloe   Oh my god.

Kev   Oh my god oh my god oh my god!

Jake   Well, this is music to my ears, I have to say.

Geoff   *Freedom!*

Kev   My mum won't have to visit me in prison!

Todd   They're not. They're really not after us.

Danny   So we're all sorted? I'll wait for my man at the stage door?

Chloe   Oh yes. Danny. I did mean to say. That man came a while back.

Danny   What? Are you serious?

Chloe   You were asleep.

Danny   OK so yeah, he's here now?

Chloe   That's right, Danny.

Geoff   The patience of a saint.

Danny   No, he hasn't. He really hasn't, that's the thing.

Chloe   Thank you for all your hard work.

Danny   Yeah, no worries.

Chloe   You did a great job!

Danny   Ace, well, I'm glad you're happy . . .

OK so yeah

my fee?

Chloe   I have been thinking, Danny. I'm not going to give you the money.

Danny   Wait no no no. A hundred. That's what you said.

Chloe   I don't think you will spend it sensibly.

Blossom   You should give it to him. He's earned it.

Chloe   But he will spend it on drugs.

Kev   Danny! No! Drugs are bad!

Jake   Chloe, maybe you have started to believe we are shiny happy learning disabled people that go around fixing everybody with our superpowers. But that's not real.

Chloe   I know that. Of course, I know that. We didn't save Joe, did we? He is still depressed, wherever he is.

Blossom   It's Danny's money. It's up to him what he spends it on.

Danny   Please, Chloe.

Chloe *takes out the cash and counts the notes. It should take as long as it takes.*

She hands over the money.

Thank you. OK so yeah. It's been.

Blossom, **Chloe**, **Geoff**, **Jake**, **Kev**, **Rose** *and* **Todd** *watch* **Danny** *leave.*

Jake (*to the audience*)   Thank you, witnesses. It appears you weren't needed after all and we have wasted your time. So I'm sorry about that.

Todd   Are you, are you OK, Kev?

Kev   I mean. Wow! Wow, guys. That was a lot. That was a lot, a lot.

Geoff   Sure was.

Kev   I think I'll just sit here for a minute, you know?

Rose   I'll do the same.

Jake   I think I'll join you.

Blossom   Let's all do that.

Blossom, **Chloe**, **Geoff**, **Jake**, **Kev**, **Rose** *and* **Todd** *sit in peaceful contemplation.*

After a while,

Todd   Ready Blossom? Ready Chloe? Ready Geoff? Ready Jake? Ready Kev? Ready Rose?

The others show **Todd** *they are ready.*

They all stand.

Chloe   Well done everyone. I think we can go home.

They exit.

THE END